REA

3·16·76

highlights of hebrew history

BOOKS BY CHARLES W. CONN

BIBLICAL

The Bible: Book of Books
A Guide to the Pentateuch
Christ and the Gospels
Acts of the Apostles
Survey of the Epistles
Highlights of Hebrew History

DEVOTIONAL

The Rudder and the Rock
A Certain Journey
The Pointed Pen

DOCTRINAL

Pillars of Pentecost
Why Men Go Back
A Balanced Church

HISTORICAL

Like a Mighty Army
Where the Saints Have Trod
The Evangel Reader

Cover design: Lonzo T. Kirkland

CHURCH TRAINING COURSE 203

Prepared under the auspices of the Church of God
General Youth and Christian Education Board

highlights of hebrew history

CHARLES W. CONN

PATHWAY PRESS, CLEVELAND, TENNESSEE

This book is dedicated with paternal love to
R. STEPHEN WESSON
PATRICIA E. MILLER
DARLIA M. MCLUHAN
DALE F. CANNON
CLAUDE R. WARREN
DONNA KAY TAYLOR
DEBORAH JOAN DAVIS
PHYLLIS ANN HUDSON

who by marriage to my children
are now my children too;
whom the Lord, the Law, and Love
have made my own.

THE CHURCH TRAINING COURSE SERIES

HIGHLIGHTS OF HEBREW HISTORY, by Charles W. Conn, has been designated in the Church Training Course program at CTC 203. A Certificate of Credit will be awarded on the basis of the following requirements:

1. The written review and instructions for preparing the review are listed on pages 111, 112. The written review must be completed and reviewed by the pastor or someone whom he may designate. Then the name of the student must be sent to the state office. (No grade will be given for the written review.)

2. The book must be read through.

3. Training sessions must be attended unless permission for absence is granted by the instructor.

4. The written review is not an examination, but is designated to review the text and to reinforce the information presented in the text. Students should search the text for the proper answers.

5. If no classes are conducted in this course of study, Church Training Course credit may be secured by home study.

A training record should be kept in the local church for each person who studies this and other courses in the Church Training Course program. A record form, CTC No. 33, will be furnished upon request from the state office.

AUTHOR'S PREFACE

In the study of the Pentateuch we left the Hebrew people wandering in the Sinai wilderness, without a land to call their own. In this study of the Historical Books we follow them into Canaan, where they carved out a homeland, and stay with them as they establish a great nation and then lose it and become a homeless people again.

The study of Old Testament history is essential to understanding and appreciation of the New Testament itself. It is easy to gain an impression that the Hebrew people experienced a long and glorious life in their homeland, which was not strictly true. Although there were long periods when the Jewish state was indeed glorious, the long history of the Hebrews is an undulating line, with many ups and downs, mountain peaks and valleys, as the people on occasion rose to greatness and just as often sank to shame.

We must remember that Israel was surrounded by pagan nations whose pernicious influences crept through the strongest barriers to corrupt the people. Only men of stedfast hearts could remain untouched, and such men were often lacking. For that reason Hebrew history is filled with accounts of both high heroics and low debauchery.

This present study begins with the establishing of a homeland under Joshua and concludes with its reestablishment, after a period of destruction and exile, under Ezra and Nehemiah. It is naturally impossible to cover such a vast amount of history briefly. This study therefore touches only the highlights of Hebrew history, those things that were of major significance in the progression of God's people. Brief and sketchy as it is, I trust that the study will be sufficient to stimulate continued and serious study of Hebrew history. No study is more interesting or pleasant.

I have found the following works very beneficial in the course of this writing: *Know Your Bible* by W. Graham Scroggie (Pickering and Inglis Ltd.), *Understanding the Books of the Old Testament* by Patrick H. Carmichael (John Knox Press), *The Kings of Israel and Judah* by George Rawlinson (Fleming H. Revell Company), *Unger's Bible Handbook* by Merrell F. Unger (Moody Press), *Introducing the Old Testament* by Clydè T. Francisco (Broadman Press), *The Story of Israel* by Stephen Szikszai (The Westminster Press), *An Outline of Old Testament History* by Charles F. Pfeiffer (Moody Press), *A Manual of Bible History* by William G. Blaikie.

* * *

Despite its brevity, and perhaps because of it, the preparation of this study has been a tedious and long drawn out task. Without the assistance and understanding of several persons it would have been even more tedious, tiring and time-consuming.

First of all, Cecil R. Guiles, General Youth and Christian Education Director, has been helpful and patient during the slow development of the manuscript.

My secretary, Mrs. Evaline Echols, has given generously of her energies and personal time to type the manuscript and attend the details of its preparation. She is due much appreciation.

Edna, my wife and chief motivator to "put pen to paper," has been most patient of all. Without the combination of her prodding and understanding I could still be wandering in the wilderness short of the promised land.

Charles W. Conn

Cleveland, Tennessee
March, 1975

Table of Contents

The I
Historical Books

Twelve of the Old Testament books are known as the "Historical Books." In Canonical sequence they follow the Pentateuch, or the Five Books of the Law, which are also largely historical in content. The Pentateuch tells of the Hebrew people before they had a homeland; the Historical Books record their history from the time they established a homeland and became a nation to the time the nation was destroyed. The record ends as the people began to restore their beloved land. In the twelve books we see Israel grow into a strong nation, and we follow the expansion of the Jewish kingdom under great leaders. This is therefore the record of Israel during its most notable period.

Other books of the Old Testament contain historical material, but these Historical Books carry the preponderant share of the record. They are almost totally historical. Spiritual lessons can be drawn from the history, but the principal purpose of the books is to record the rise and fall of the Jewish nation. The spiritual lessons were drawn by the prophets in their writings of each period.

Dating the events of the Old Testament is difficult, especially the early periods before the days of the kings. There are scientific approaches to the effort but even the best of these are neither precise nor consistent. According to a commonly accepted chronology, the Historical Books cover a period of about 1,055 years, dating from the death of Moses to the close of the Old Testament. This is a long period, which can be divided into three main parts, first, from the death of Moses to the accession of Saul, 355 years; second, from the accession of Saul to the overthrow of Judah, 510 years; and third, from the overthrow of Judah to the end of Old Testament history, 190 years. By getting that perspective it will be easier to follow the unfolding story. These periods represent three forms of Hebrew government, first the Theocracy, or rule of God; second the Monarchy, or rule of kings; and third, the Dependency, or rule of alien nations. Now let us look at this division in outline form:

> Joshua to Saul, 355 years
> Saul to Fall of Judah, 510 years
> Fall of Judah to end of Old Testament, 190 years

In order to fix the twelve Historical Books in mind we need to view the entire list in their sequence.

> Joshua
> Judges
> Ruth
> 1 and 2 Samuel
> 1 and 2 Kings
> 1 and 2 Chronicles
> Ezra
> Nehemiah
> Esther

Of this list, three record the early history of the Jewish nation; six record the history of the nation when it was ruled by kings, and three record historic aspects of the captivity.

EARLY HISTORY
Joshua, Judges, Ruth

THE MONARCHY
1 and 2 Samuel
1 and 2 Kings
1 and 2 Chronicles

THE CAPTIVITY
Ezra, Nehemiah, Esther

Now let us look at the list in sequence:

JOSHUA
JUDGES   The early history
                              of Israel

RUTH   **Early historic interlude**

1 SAMUEL   History of the monarchy
2 SAMUEL   during the United Kingdom

1 KINGS   History of the divided Kingdom,
2 KINGS   Israel and Judah

1 CHRONICLES   History of David and the
2 CHRONICLES   kings of Judah

EZRA   History of Judah during
NEHEMIAH   the Captivity

ESTHER   **Interlude of the Captivity**

Viewed as a historical unit, the twelve Historical Books are as follows:

The Book of Joshua

The Book of Joshua follows the Pentateuch and concludes the story of how God delivered His people from Egypt. What Moses began when he led the Israelites out of slavery, Joshua continued and completed. He led the people in the conquest of Canaan and divided the land among the tribes of Israel as their homeland. The book bears the name of Joshua because he is the principal character in it. It is generally regarded that Joshua himself was author of the book, but no one can ever really be sure of that. The book is a vital link between the Pentateuch and the further history of Israel. It is in it that we have the conclusion of the Hebrews' exodus from Egypt and the establishment of their own national identity.

Outline of Joshua

I. *The Hebrews Enter Canaan (1:1-5:15)*

   A. The Appointment of Joshua (1:1-18)

   B. The Role of Rahab (2:1-24)

   C. Crossing of the Jordan River (3:1-4:24)

   D. Encampment at Gilgal (5:1-12)

   E. "Captain of the Lord's Host" (5:13-15)

II. *The Conquest of Canaan (6:1-12:24)*

   A. The Fall of Jericho (6:1-27)

The Book of Judges

This is the record of Israel's early years in their national homeland. In that primitive period all of those who had participated in the exodus from Egypt and the conquest of Canaan disappeared from the scene and leadership of the nation passed into other hands. Those were confused and uncertain days in Jewish history, and

the Book of Judges is a graphic account of the young
nation's troubles and failures. The period was punctu-
ated by a dreary succession of apostacies by Israel, each
followed by invasion and oppression by a neighboring
enemy. In those years Israel had no king or permanent
leader, and national crises were met by men divinely en-
dowed to lead the nation. These men and one woman
were known as "judges," from which the book gets its
name. There are thirteen judges mentioned in the book,
but none continued to lead the nation on a permanent
basis; each returned to private life as soon as his crisis
was over.

Outline of Judges

I. *Israel Corrupted By the Canaanites (1:1-2:15)*

    A. Israel's Incomplete Victories (1:1-36)

    B. Israel's Spiritual Defeat (2:1-15)

II. *History of the Thirteen Judges (2:16-16:31)*

    A. Condition of the Times (2:16-3:7)

    B. Othniel, the First Judge (3:8-11)

    C. Ehud Against the Moabites (3:12-30)

    D. Shamgar and the Philistines (3:31)

    E. Deborah and Barak, Co-Judges (4:1-5:31)

    F. Gideon and the Midianites (6:1-8:35)

    G. Usurpation of Gideon's Son, Abimelech (9:1-
       57)

    H. Tola, the Seventh Judge (10:1, 2)

The Book of Ruth

This small book is not part of the mainstream of Jewish history. It is a historic sidelight, an account of domestic life during the period of the Judges. Frequently called the most beautiful story in the world, Ruth is a narrative of how one Jewish family faced difficulty, and in the telling of that story we get some of our finest views of Jewish customs in that period. The book is named for its principal character, a Moabitess named Ruth. Some of the highest spiritual example anywhere in Scripture is found in this idyllic interlude of faith and loyalty.

Outline of Ruth

I. *An Israelite Family in Moab (1:1-22)*

    A. The Tragedy in Moab (1:1-5)

    B. Naomi Returns to Bethlehem (1:6-22)

II. *A Moabitess in Israel (2:1-4:22)*

    A. Ruth Meets Boaz (2:1-23)

    B. Ruth Pledges Herself to Boaz (3:1-18)

    C. Boaz Redeems and Marries Ruth (4:1-13)

III. *The Moabitess Blesses Israel (4:14-22)*

    A. Ruth Blesses Naomi (4:14-17)

    B. Ruth Blesses All Israel (4:18-22)

The Books of Samuel

Presumably written by the prophet Samuel, who was also the fifteenth and final judge, the two books of Samuel were originally a single book. This was divided in the Septuagint (the early Greek translation of the Old Testament) as 1 Samuel and 2 Samuel, which are the history of the united kingdom of Israel. In 1 Samuel we get to the basic and formal records of Jewish history. The book begins as the period of the Judges comes to an end, and records the institution of kings who ruled over Israel. The establishment of a monarchy was not easy after the Jews had only known the rule of God (a Theocracy) before. First Samuel carries the history forward through the reign of Saul (the first king) and ends with his death. The youthful David is prominent in the record.

Second Samuel, being the second half of a continuous work, commences where 1 Samuel ends. David becomes the king of Israel and reigns over the entire kingdom of the Jews. He led Israel to national greatness. In 2 Samuel the Jews capture Jerusalem and it becomes their civil and spiritual center. In many ways the book is a record of Israel's most glorious age: under David the kingdom advanced at home and abroad.

Outline of 1 and 2 Samuel

I. *Samuel, Last of the Judges (1 Samuel 1:1-7:17)*

A. The Birth of Samuel (1:1-2:11)

B. The Failure of Eli (2:12-36)

C. The Call of Samuel (3:1-21)

D. Capture and Recovery of the Ark (4:1-7:2)

E. Victory Over the Philistines (7:3-17)

II. *Saul, First King of Israel (1 Samuel 8:1-14:52)*

A. Israel Demands a King (8:1-22)

B. Saul Anointed King (9:1-10:27)

C. Early Successes of Saul (11:1-12:25)

D. Saul's Disobedience and Self-Will (13:1-15)

E. Jonathan Defeats the Philistines (13:16-14:52)

F. Saul's Rejection as King (15:1-35)

III. *David's Preparation for Kingship (1 Samuel 16:1-31:13)*

A. David Anointed to Be King (16:1-23)

B. The Contest With Goliath (17:1-54)

C. David in the Court of Saul (17:55-19:17)

   1. Friendship With Jonathan (18:1-7)

   2. Marriage to Michal (18:20-28)

D. David Flees From Saul (19:18-20:42)

E. Exile and Preservation (21:1-30:31)

F. Death of Saul and His Sons (31:1-13)

IV. *David, King of Judah and Israel (2 Samuel 1:1-10:19)*

A. Mourning for Saul and Jonathan (1:1-27)

B. David Anointed King of Judah (2:1-7)

C. Pretension of Ishbosheth (2:8-4:12)

D. David Anointed King of Israel (5:1-5)

E. Jerusalem Becomes the National Center (5:6-7:29)

F. The Kingdom Is Expanded (8:1-10:19)

V. *David's Sin and Its Consequences (2 Samuel 11:1-19:8)*

A. David and Bathsheba (11:1-27)

B. David's Repentance (12:1-23)

C. The Birth of Solomon (12:24, 25)

D. Ammon's Incestuous Sin (13:1-39)

E. The Rebellion of Absalom (14:1-19:8)

VI. *The Last Days of David (2 Samuel 19:9-24:25)*

   A. Return to Jerusalem (19:9-40)

   B. Israel Revolts Against David (19:41-20:26)

   C. Famine and War (21:1-22)

   D. David's Testimony and Devotion (22:1-24:25)

The Books of Kings

The two books of Kings and the two of Samuel are one continuous history of Israel. And so 1 Kings begins where 2 Samuel ends, with an account of the last days of David's reign. When David died, his son Solomon became king. Under his rule Israel's empire was spread to its greatest extent. But 1 Kings records the end of the united kingdom, because the nation was divided into two kingdoms at the death of Solomon. The northern kingdom would ever after be known as Israel and the southern kingdom as Judah. The book of 1 Kings records the early history of the divided kingdom and the hostility that existed between the two sections. The account of the kings who acceded to the throne of each kingdom becomes a monotony of evil and failure.

We also read in 1 Kings of the mighty ministry of Elijah, possibly the greatest prophet of the Old Testament. He was like a spiritual peak towering above a wilderness of evil.

Second Kings begins where 1 Kings ends and carries the parallel history of the divided kingdom forward to each kingdom's time of ruin and captivity. The northern kingdom of Israel was destroyed first by Assyria, and the southern kingdom of Judah continued alone for al-

most 150 years, when it was also defeated by Babylon.
First Kings begins with the united kingdom at the
height of its glory and 2 Kings ends with the kingdom
divided and both divisions defeated and in captivity to
alien powers. Within four hundred years the Jewish
people went from the height of their glory to the depths
of failure.

The great ministry of Elisha, successor to Elijah, is
recorded in 2 Kings. The wonderful miracles performed
by him are a bright spot in an otherwise bleak period of
Jewish history.

Outline of 1 and 2 Kings

I. *Solomon and the United Kingdom (1 Kings 1:1-11:43)*

    A. The Decline of David (1:1-38)

    B. Solomon Is Anointed King (1:39-53)

    C. David's Last Words and Death (2:1-11)

    D. Solomon Eliminates His Opponents (2:12-46)

    E. The Wisdom of Solomon (3:1-28)

    F. Consolidation of the Kingdom (4:1-34)

    G. Building Projects of Solomon (5:1-9:28)

    H. The Queen of Sheba (10:1-29)

    I. Solomon's Apostasy and Death (11:1-43)

II. *Judah and Israel Divided (1 Kings 12:1-22:53)*

    A. The Kingdom Is Split (12:1-14:31)

A. The Reign of Hezekiah (18:1-20:21)

B. Manasseh and Amon of Judah (21:1-26)

C. The Reformation Under Josiah (22:1-23:30)

D. The Last Days of Judah (23:31-37)

E. Judah Defeated and Deported (24:1-25:30)

The Books of Chronicles

Like Samuel and Kings, the Books of Chronicles were originally one book; this single book was divided into two by the translators of the Septuagint. It is commonly believed that Chronicles was written by Ezra as part of a history of the Hebrews, the other parts being Ezra and Nehemiah. The work is a repetition of what is recorded in 2 Samuel and the Books of Kings. The focus is almost entirely upon the reign of David and his descendants, who ruled over the Kingdom of Judah. Little attention is given to the Northern Kingdom. The historical narrative of 1 Chronicles begins with the accession of David to the throne and concludes with his death and the accession of Solomon. The books amount to a retelling of the life of the great king.

In 2 Chronicles the history of the Southern Kingdom of Judah is continued from the glorious reign of Solomon to the time of the Jewish defeat and captivity. The Northern Kingdom of Israel receives only passing attention, for only the Davidic line was regarded as representing the true Israel. As a matter of spiritual interpretation, the apostasy of Judah is seen as the reason for the nation's overthrow and captivity. The book concludes with an account of Judah defeated and existing only as a vassal state to enemy powers.

Outline of 1 and 2 Chronicles

I. *Genealogies of the Hebrews (1 Chronicles 1:1-9:44)*

    A. The Patriarchs (1:1-54)

    B. The Line of Judah (2:1-4:23)

    C. The Line of Simeon (4:24-43)

    D. Reuben, Gad and Manasseh (5:1-26)

    E. Genealogy of Levi (6:1-81)

    F. Other Tribal Genealogies (7:1-40)

    G. The Lines of Judah and Benjamin (8:1-9:44)

II. *The Reign of David (1 Chronicles 10:1-29:30)*

    A. The Death of Saul (10:1-14)

    B. David and His Mighty Men (11:1-12:40)

    C. Search for the Ark (13:1-14)

    D. Victory Over the Philistines (14:1-17)

    E. The Ark Brought to Jerusalem (15:1-16:43)

    F. David's Desire to Build a Temple (17:1-27)

    G. His Wars and Conquests (18:1-20:8)

III. *The Latter Days of David (1 Chronicles 21:1-29:30)*

    A. His Sin of Numbering the People (21:1-30)

    B. The Rise of Solomon (22:1-19)

    C. The Priestly Organization (23:1-26:32)

    D. The Civil Organization (27:1-34)

The Book of Ezra

Jewish history did not end with the Captivity. The Book of Ezra tells how a priest by that name led a contingent of Jews back to Jerusalem to rebuild the Temple. Zerubbabel was enthroned as vassal king, subservient to Persian rule. The heroic events of the book show the tenacity of faith and the courageous character of the Jewish people. The Temple was restored and worship was resumed in it.

Outline of Ezra

I. *First Return of Exiles to Jerusalem (1:1-2:70)*

   A. The Proclamation of Cyrus (1:1-4)

   B. Preparation for the Return (1:5-11)

   C. Register of Those Who Returned (2:1-70)

II. *Restoration of Worship in Jerusalem (3:1-6:22)*

   A. The Altar Is Rebuilt (3:1-7)

   B. The Temple Foundation Rebuilt (3:8-13)

   C. Work Hindered and Stopped (4:1-24)

      1. The Samaritans' Offer to Help (4:1-4)

      2. Complaint to Artaxerxes (4:5-24)

   D. Work on the Temple Is Resumed (5:1-6:12)

   E. The Temple Completed, Dedicated (6:13-22)

III. *Ezra's Return and Reformation (7:1-10:44)*

A. Ezra Commissioned to Return (7:1-28)

B. The Return to Jerusalem (8:1-36)

C. Ezra Leads Spiritual Reformation (9:1-10:44)

    1. Mixed Marriages Denounced (9:1-15)

    2. The People Are Restored (10:1-44)

The Book of Nehemiah

This book seems also to have been written by Ezra, and it tells of Jewish courage and faith. What Ezra did to restore the spiritual life of Judah, Nehemiah did to restore civil life. Under his leadership the walls of Jerusalem, which had been broken down during the Babylonian conquest, were rebuilt. Both Ezra and Nehemiah give pathetic pictures of a nation that once was great but had fallen under enemy rule. Yet the two books are narratives of how faith and spiritual loyalty live stubbornly in the face of adversity and opposition.

Outline of Nehemiah

I. *Nehemiah's Return to Jerusalem (1:1-2:20)*

    A. Sad News From Jerusalem (1:1-4)

    B. Nehemiah's Prayer for the City (1:5-11)

    C. The Request to Return (2:1-10)

    D. Nehemiah at the Broken Walls (2:11-20)

II. *The Building of the Walls (3:1-7:4)*

    A. The Builders and Their Work (3:1-32)

The Book of Esther

Last of the Historical Books is the story of a woman of courage during the captivity in Persia. The story of Esther unfolded in the courts of Persia during the period Ezra and Nehemiah were in Jerusalem. Like the Book of Ruth, Esther has little significance to the mainstream of Jewish history. It is a valorous episode in the life of certain Jewish people. The book shows the customs of its day in the same way Ruth did the customs of that day. No book of the Old Testament more clearly reveals God's watchcare over His people.

Outline of Esther

C. Esther Is Chosen to Be Queen (2:1-23)

II. *The Divine Purpose of Esther (3:1-8:17)*

    A. Haman's Plot Against the Jews (3:1-15)

    B. Mordecai Appeals to Esther for Help (4:1-17)

    C. Esther Intervenes for Her People (5:1-1/4)

    D. The Execution of Haman (6:1-7:10)

    E. Protection Provided for the Jews (8:1-17)

III. *Results of Esther's Appeal (9:1-10:3)*

    A. The Jewish Victory (9:1-19)

    B. Feast of Purim Instituted (9:20-32)

    C. Mordecai's Post of Honor (10:1-3)

QUESTIONS AND REVIEW

1. What are the "Historical Books"?
2. Can you name them in their order?
3. Where are they located in Scripture?
4. What books were named for women?
5. Which three books were of early Hebrew history?
6. Which three are books of the Captivity?
7. Who were the Judges? Were they permanent or temporary?
8. How much time do the Historical Books 'cover?
9. Why is the study of these books important to us?
10. Can you give a general idea of what is recorded in each book?

Conquering 2
a Homeland

Read Joshua 1-24

🐾 After spending a generation in the Sinai wilderness, the Hebrews reached the Jordan River, beyond which lay the land of Canaan. Canaan, the former home of Abraham, Isaac and Jacob, had often been promised to the descendants of Abraham, which the Hebrews were. Their forty years of wandering had doubtlessly made the people hungry for a land of their own; and now that land was in view. During their forty years in the wilderness the Israelites had acquired a system of laws, an administrative government, and a mode of worship. Their one need now was a land in which to establish themselves as a nation.

Moses, the great leader of Israel, was not permitted by the Lord to lead the people into Canaan. He died and was buried on Mount Nebo in the land of Moab. Moses' death was nothing less than a tragedy to the people. He had brought them out of Egypt, given them the Law, led them through the wilderness, and had been both spiritual and civil leader for forty years. He was the only leader the people now alive could remember.

The responsibility of leading the people into Canaan was entrusted to a comrade of Moses named Joshua. He was a natural choice to direct the invasion, for he had served as the military leader of Israel's battles in the wilderness (Exodus 17:8-10, 13); he was one of the men who spied out the land of Canaan for Moses (Numbers 13:16; 14:6, 30); and he was Moses' constant companion in labor and service (Exodus 24:13; 32:17; 33:11).

Joshua was first presented as Moses' successor while Israel was still in the wilderness (Numbers 27:15-20), where God Himself "gave Joshua the son of Nun a charge, and said, Be strong and of a good courage: for thou shalt bring the children of Israel into the land which I sware unto them: and I will be with thee" (Deuteronomy 31:23).

The Invasion

Joshua sent two spies into Jericho, a walled city located across the Jordan River from the Hebrew encampment. This strong city would be the first to be attacked by the Hebrews when they began their invasion. The spies were assisted by a harlot named Rahab, who had heard how the Red Sea opened for the Israelites and of the Hebrew victories over the desert kingdoms. Rahab lived on the walls of Jericho; the vast walls of cities were sometimes utilized with apartments that helped house the people of the city. She hid the spies from detection and then helped them escape their pursuers.

Because she risked her own life to help the spies escape capture, Rahab's life was spared when the Hebrews attacked. Because of her faith in the God of Israel she is listed among the heroines of faith in the Epistle to the Hebrews (11:31). Although she was a heathen and a harlot, she joined the Hebrew cause and became the wife of Salmon and the mother of Boaz, and thereby one of the ancestors of Jesus Christ (Matthew 1:5).

The spies reported to Joshua that they had learned that the people of Jericho were afraid of them "Truly the Lord hath delivered into our hands all the land; for even all the inhabitants of the country do faint because of us" (2:24). Three days later the Hebrews crossed the Jordan River into Canaan. Their journey that began forty years earlier with a miraculous crossing of the Red Sea ended with a miraculous crossing of the Jordan River. When the priests who led the procession stepped into the water the river dried up under their feet. Exactly how the miracle occurred is not specified, but the language used (3:13, 16) suggests that the river was dammed up by a landslide upstream from where they crossed. When the river was blocked upstream, the water downstream drained away until there was a large dry place, sufficient for the two million Hebrews to pass over. **1902876**

After the crossing the Lord commanded the people to make a pillar of twelve stones on each side of the river. This was to remind the Hebrews thereafter of how God had led their forefathers across Jordan on dry land.

Israel camped in the plains west of Jordan, and called the place "Gilgal," which means "A Rolling," for God "rolled away the reproach of Egypt" from them. At Gilgal the males were circumcised, for this rite had not been practiced in the wilderness and the people celebrated the Passover, which had not been observed since they left Egypt. The manna that had fallen from heaven in Sinai was stopped; the people instead ate the provisions of the land. Traces of Egypt and the Sinai wilderness were wiped away, for now the "land of milk and honey" was within their reach.

Joshua received dramatic reassurance and confirmation of victory when a man with an unsheathed sword appeared to him as the Hebrew host advanced toward Jericho. Joshua, understandably concerned about the coming battle, feared that the armed man might be hostile to the Hebrews. "Are you with us, or with our enemies?" he asked. The man replied, "I am the captain of the Lord's host." Recognizing the divine character of the stranger, Joshua worshipped him. The message was clear: the forthcoming battle would be fought by the Lord. The victory would belong to God, not to the military might of the Hebrews. The Lord said, "See, I have given into thy hand Jericho, and the king thereof, and the mighty men of valour" (6:2).

The Central Highlands

From a natural point of view, the idea that the Israelites, however brave they were, could defeat the walled cities of Canaan was absurd. The Canaanites were prepared for war, fortified against attack and equipped with chariots, horses of war and well-trained armies. The Hebrews had no chariots, no beasts of battle, no swordsmen and no professional army. It was incomprehensible that such a rag-tag army could take a powerful city such as Jericho.

God directed the people to march around the city

once each day for six days. Seven men with trumpets of rams' horns would lead the procession, followed by priests bearing the ark of the covenant, and then by the soldiers. On the seventh day they were to circle the city seven times, and then the seven trumpeters were to blow their trumpets and the people were to shout loudly. The directions were followed, with the Hebrews returning each night to their camp at Gilgal. At the blast of the trumpets and the shout of the people on the seventh day a great miracle happened—"the wall fell down flat" (6:20). The Hebrews rushed into the city amid the inevitable confusion and destroyed the city and its inhabitants. Only Rahab and her family were spared. The overthrow of Jericho was a notable victory, and the news of it spread throughout Canaan. The strong and ancient city was taken without a fight, and the people who were once secure behind their strong walls were all killed by the sword of Israel.

The riches of the city were taken for the Lord's use. No man was allowed to take spoil for himself, everything was to be consecrated to the Lord.

Following Jericho, the Hebrews attacked Ai, a town so lightly defended that Joshua led only 3000 men against it. Ai should have been conquered easily. Instead, the Israelites were defeated and thirty-six of them were killed. Joshua was distraught, fearful that the defeat would demoralize Israel and encourage their enemies. God revealed to Joshua that one of his men had sinned, and that this sin was responsible for the defeat of the entire body.

Achan, one of the Hebrews, had violated the commandment of God at Jericho. Even though the spoil of the city was consecrated to God's service, he had taken a gold wedge and other items for himself. As it often happens in life, many people suffered because of the sin of one. Achan was stoned to death, a common form of punishment at that time. The lessons of this episode would never be forgotten by Israel; and the case of Achan is important to us today.

Ai was then taken by the Hebrews, who went against the city in greater force. Five thousand men lay in ambush near the city while a second force attacked it. When the defenders of Ai went out to fight the at-tackers, the 5000 men that lay in ambush stormed the city and destroyed it. Then the two Hebrew forces joined in the defeat of the army of Ai. This was a clever military strategem and word of another Hebrew victory created even greater fear among the inhabitants of Canaan.

Joshua dramatized the Hebrews' dependency upon God by erecting an altar upon Mount Ebal, near Shechem in central Palestine. The Law was then read to the people to remind them of their responsibility to God. Following their victories at Jericho and Ai, and the dreadful example of Achan, the people needed to under-stand that obedience of the Law would bring them blessings and disobedience would bring punishment.

Another group of people living in the central high-lands of Palestine were the Gibeonites. Hearing of the Hebrew victories in Jericho and Ai, they feared for their lives and devised a treaty with the Hebrews. The Gibeonites sent messengers to Joshua in Gilgal pretend-ing to be ambassadors from a distant land. To make their ruse more convincing, the messengers dressed as if they were travel-worn from a long journey. The decep-tion worked and Joshua formed an alliance with the

Gibeonites. Three days later the deception was discovered, but Israel honored the treaty and did not attack Gibeonite cities. Instead, the Gibeonites were made slaves as punishment for their deceit.

Later events would prove Joshua wrong in sparing the Gibeonites, and other people of Canaan. These were heathen people who soon corrupted the Israelites and conditioned them for apostasy.

The Southern Campaign

The Gibeonite alliance with the Hebrews was a major disappointment to the Amorites of southern Palestine. Gibeon was a powerful city, one the people of Canaan had hoped would repel the Hebrew invasion. Fear and anger prompted a quick confederation of five cities. Led by Adoni-Zedec, king of Jerusalem, they joined together and set out to punish the Gibeonites. According to terms of the alliance, the Gibeonites sent to Gilgal to ask Joshua for help. Joshua rushed by night to Gibeon's defense. The confederate army fled northward in disarray, with the Israelites in hot pursuit. Nature became Joshua's ally, when a storm came and hailstones fell on the fleeing Amorites and killed more than had died in battle.

It was in the battle that followed the hailstorm that Joshua commanded the sun to stand still. Evidently the day was drawing to a close before Joshua was able to complete the victory that was imminent. "So the sun stood still in the midst of heaven, and hasted not to go down about a whole day" (10:13). Joshua won a decisive victory over the armies, then turned southward and destroyed the Amorite cities. All of Southern Palestine was then under Hebrew control.

The Northern Campaign

Then the Israelites faced a new confederacy in the north. Jabin, king of Hazor, attempted what the southern confederacy was unable to do. He organized a host of warriors from among the Canaanites, Amorites, Hittites, Perizzites, Jebusites, and Hivites, and set out to destroy the Hebrews. Joshua attacked the vast army boldly and won a decisive victory.

Defeat of the northern opposition ended the major campaign against Canaan. Organized resistance to Israel ended with the battle at Merom. Full conquest was not realized; large pockets of resistance remained to plague the Hebrews for years to come. This situation would continue throughout the period of the Judges. Yet, for all practical purposes the northern campaign ended the conquest of Canaan.

Joshua 11:16-12:34 gives a summary of the victories won by both Moses and Joshua. It is an impressive list, one that shows the way God guides those who are yielded to Him. The conquest saw many miracles that brought glory and victory to Israel, for the battle was the Lord's.

The Tribal Allotments

Joshua 13-24 records the routine and rather mundane allotment of the conquered territory to the twelve tribes of Israel. The Canaanites were still undefeated in some important places—especially along the Mediterranean coast north and south. Yet there should be no further delay in the assignment of territory to the tribes. Moses had permitted Reuben, Gad and half the tribe of Manasseh to claim the eastern side of the Jordan River as their territory. These came into the western section to assist the remaining tribes in the Conquest, but eastern Palestine remained their designated land.

Caleb and Joshua were the only two who survived the wilderness wandering and entered Canaan. In apportioning the western territory, the promise of Moses to Caleb was remembered (Deuteronomy 1:36). With this special apportionment satisfied, the tribes of Israel were assigned to their territory. The accompanying map will show the general area of these allocations.

As specified in the Mosaic law (Numbers 35), six cities of refuge were established as sanctuaries for anyone guilty of unintentional murder. A man who unintentionally killed another could take refuge in one of the cities, thereby escaping the hasty vengeance of a grieved relative until he was able to have a fair trial. Three cities of refuge were designated for eastern Palestine and three for the western territory, so all Israel would have easy access to needed sanctuary.

The tribe of Levi would have no territorial assignment, for the Levites were the priests of Israel and would be scattered throughout the land. Certain cities were assigned to them for convenience to the nation. Then the three tribes of Reuben, Gad and Manasseh returned to their new land on the east of Jordan.

When Joshua became very old and knew he would soon die he reviewed to the elders of Israel how God had called him to lead the conquest of Canaan. He reminded the people of how God had dealt with Moses and Aaron before him. Then Joshua died in Shechem at the great age of 110 years. He had accomplished a great work for God, and the Israelites were at long last settled in their promised land.

QUESTIONS FOR REVIEW

1. How long did the Israelites wander in the wilderness before entering Canaan?

2. What was the cause of this period of wandering?

3. Who led in the conquest of Canaan?

4. Who was Rahab? How was she blessed for her assistance to the Hebrews?

5. What miracle occurred as the Hebrews crossed the Jordan River?

6. What was the sin of Achan? What was the consequence of his sin?

7. In what way did the Gibeonites deceive Joshua?

8. Why did Joshua command the sun to stand still?

9. In what way did the Hebrews disobey God's commandment regarding the conquest of Canaan? How did this later affect them?

10. Name the twelve tribes of Israel. Give a general idea of the location of each tribe in the distribution of land following the conquest.

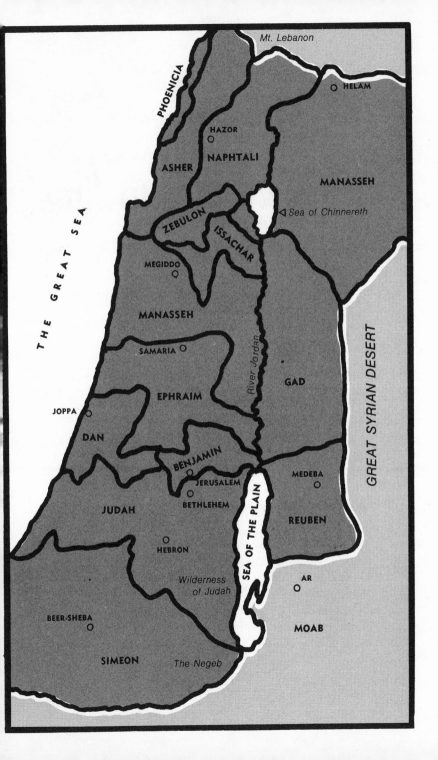

"The Lord   3
Raised Up Judges"

Read Judges 1-21

Following the initial conquest of Canaan many pockets of resistance remained among or alongside the Israelites. The book of Judges opens with an account of efforts by individual tribes to defeat the remaining Canaanite strongholds. There is no indication that the Hebrews sought to destroy the enemies. This was a mistake, for the Canaanites would live like thorns in their sides, and the thorns would one day fester and contaminate the nation of Israel. Six times in chapter one we are told of Israel's incomplete victories (1:19, 21, 27, 30, 32, 33). The defeated people were subjugated but not destroyed, and in time they came to be acceptable neighbors who influenced Israel more than they were influenced by them.

This military compromise sowed the seed of spiritual failure. While Joshua lived, the people maintained a measure of obedience to the laws of God. When he died, and his generation with him, there remained little remembrance of God and His wonderful works. The Hebrews intermarried with the heathenish people of Canaan, and gradually adopted their idolatrous practices.

44

"And they forsook the Lord, and served Baal and Ash-taroth" (2:13). Baal worship was cruel, frequently savage, and involved great indignity and reprobation. Ashtaroth was a goddess of lust and impurity, wor-shiped by overt acts of indecency and licentiousness.

The New Leaders

Until the death of Joshua the Hebrews had a leader whom God specifically called and ordained for leader-ship; first, Moses, then Joshua. But no one was appoint-ed to take Joshua's place. There was no single person or place to give the people a sense of unity. Each tribe was its own entity, and the twelve were yet to be welded into a united nation. Just as each tribe operated alone, so "every man did that which was right in his own eyes" (17:6).

Disorder was inevitable. The people adopted the evil practices of their neighbors, for which they suffered greatly. The pattern we see throughout the book of Judges is this: (1) First, the people forsook God; (2) then God punished them by allowing an enemy to oppress them; (3) which resulted in repentance and prayer for deliverance; (4) which God answered by raising up a leader to deliver them.

There were seven periods of apostasy, with seven times of oppression, and seven occasions of deliverance. Thir-teen judges were raised up to meet the need, but few of them were permanent and none ever set up a dynasty or was succeeded by an heir to his judgeship. The word "judge" was not used in the sense that we think of today. Rather than national judiciary officials or administrators, the judges were local chieftans who rallied the people of his particular tribe to repel their oppressor. All twelve of the tribes never united under a leader, but only the one tribe affected, or those few other tribes who chose to cooperate. Some of the judges were contemporaries; two or more may well have worked at the same time in different sections of the nation. If the years the judges ruled were consecutive, the period would be about 400 years. That is not likely. The period of the judges, allowing for the difficulties of chronological computation, was probably nearer 300 years.

Othniel

Othniel, the nephew of Caleb, was the first judge. His service came as a result of Israel's first widespread apostasy, for which they were punished with light years of bondage to the king of Mesopotamia. When the children of Israel repented of their idolatry, God raised up Othniel to deliver them. "The Spirit of the Lord came upon him, and he judged Israel, and went out to war" (3:10). Othniel's campaign was successful, and Israel enjoyed forty years of peace.

Ehud

After Othniel's death, the pattern of apostasy, punishment, repentance and deliverance began anew. Because of Israel's sins, Eglon, the king of Moab, with the assistance of the Ammonites, was enabled to conquer and enslave the Hebrews around the region of Ephraim. This servitude lasted for eighteen years before Ehud, of the tribe of Benjamin, rose up and delivered the people.

Ehud conveyed Israel's tribute, or tax, to Eglon in Moab.
When the two men were alone Ehud, who was left-
handed, assassinated Eglon, who was a very fat man,
by thrusting a dagger into his belly (3:15-29). Ehud
escaped and rallied the tribe of Ephraim, who invaded
Moab and killed 10,000 soldiers of the Moabite army.
Israel then had eighty years of rest.

Shamgar

The Philistines were the next enemies to oppress Israel. During their occupation it became dangerous to use
the regular roads so the Hebrews had to travel through
fields and byways instead (5:6). Nothing is told of the
third judge, Shamgar, except that in the course of de-
livering Israel he slew 600 Philistines with an ox goad,
a long metal-tipped pole for prodding oxen. This indi-
cates that Shamgar was a man of tremendous physical
strength.

Deborah and Barak

Once again the Israelites resorted to evil. God punished them by allowing them to be enslaved by Jabin,
the king of Canaan. For twenty years they were cruelly
treated, especially by Sisera, captain of the Canaanite
army, who had 900 chariots under his command. Deborah, a prophetess and judge at the time, appointed Barak
to help her deliver Israel from Jabin and Sisera. Deborah was a remarkable woman, who inspired Barak to
gather an army of 10,000 men from the tribes of Naphthali and Zebulun. This army gathered at Mount Tabor
in the mountains of Samaria where it defeated Sisera, with

his chariot horde. Sisera did not die in battle but was
killed by a woman named Jael as he slept in her tent trying to escape from the Israelites. She drove a tent peg
through the head of the sleeping captain (4:21). Following this deliverance from the Canaanites, Israel had
forty years of peace.

Gideon

Greatest of the judges was Gideon, who came to leadership when Israel had been in severe bondage to the
Midianites for seven years. Gideon was from Ophrah, a
city of Manasseh located sixteen miles north of Jericho.
Gideon was threshing wheat when an angel appeared to
him and called him to deliver Israel. Being a humble
man, Gideon questioned his ability to accomplish such
a task, whereupon God assured him, "Surely I will be
with thee, and thou shalt smite the Midianites as one
man" (6:16).

Gideon began his work by building an altar to the
Lord and destroying an altar of Baal that stood on his
father's property. The spiritual climate was so wretched
that Gideon, fearing reprisals by the townspeople, or even
his father's household, tore the altar down at night. The
people indeed were angry that Baal's altar was destroyed and they contended with Gideon's father, Joash,
about the matter. They wanted to kill Gideon.

Sensing that Gideon was intent upon driving them
out of Israel, the Midianites, along with their allies, the
Amalekites, prepared for battle and camped in the valley of Jezreel. Gideon sent messengers to the tribes of
Asher, Zebulun and Naphthali, calling them together to

save Israel. Thousands of men responded to his call; in fact, so many responded that all of them could not be used.

Gideon thinned his army down to a mere 300 so they and all Israel would have to know that it was God and not their own power that delivered them from Midian. The final method of elimination concerned the manner in which the people drank water. Three hundred (300) were so eager for the battle that they scooped water into their hands and lapped it as they prepared to attack.

The 300 were divided into three companies who used trumpets, torches and empty pitchers to confuse the Midianites and win one of the most famous victories in Hebrew history. The land was "in quietness forty years in the days of Gideon" (8:28).

When Gideon died "in a good old age" one of his seventy sons, Abimelech, attempted to set himself up as king. Abimelech killed his brothers (or half-brothers, since Gideon had many wives) and reigned as king for three years. Abimelech was killed as he tried to secure himself as king. The time for dynasties in Israel had not yet come.

Tola

Tola was the next judge, but little is told about him except that he was of the tribe of Issachar, lived in Ephraim, and judged Israel twenty-three years (10:1, 2).

Jair

Jair, a man of Gilead, next judged Israel for twenty-two years. He had thirty sons who rode on thirty ass colts and were the leaders of thirty villages of Gilead, a land east of the Jordan River. Riding an ass colt was a sign of authority and affluence.

Jephthah

One of the most pathetic incidents of Hebrew history concerned Jephthah, the ninth judge. A Gileadite, he was called to deliver Israel from servitude to the Ammonites and the Philistines, an oppression that lasted eighteen years. Jephthah had an unhappy background. The illegitimate son of a harlot, he was cast out of his father's house by his brethren. He thereupon went to the land of Tob, where he associated with a band of desperadoes. This was his circumstance when the men of Gilead called on him to fight the Ammonites.

During the battle against the Ammonites Jephthah rashly vowed to sacrifice as a burnt offering the first thing that greeted him when he returned home. Tragically, it was his only child, a daughter, not a ram or goat or bullock, that met him. Jephthah kept his vow, but there is some uncertainty about how it was done. The earliest interpretation was that the daughter was literally offered as a "burnt offering," according to the terms of Jephthah's vow (11:31). Later interpretation is that the daughter was dedicated to the service of God, and lived her lifetime unmarried and isolated from the world. If the former were correct, there would be much difficulty in understanding how a champion of Israel could resort to human sacrifice, one of the most terrible evils of the people whom he defeated. It was human sacrifice in the "high places" of heathen worship that made them so abominable to the Lord. The Hebrews were to stamp it out, not practice it. It is a much more humane and reasonable interpretation that Jephthah's daughter remained a virgin, dedicated to God's service in some way apart from the world. Each year the women of Gilead spent four days lamenting the unhappy situation created by Jephthah's rash vow (11:37-40).

Jephthah judged Israel only six years, and this brief time was further saddened by a war between Gilead and the tribe of Ephraim. The war was over Ephraim's complaint that they were not involved in the war against the Ammonites (12:1). It was a bitter inter-tribal conflict that emphasizes the disunity of the times.

Ibzan

Ibzan, of Bethlehem, was the tenth judge, but nothing is known of him except that he had thirty sons and thirty daughters (12:9). He gave his daughters in marriage to men outside Bethlehem, and arranged for his sons to marry girls from outside Bethlehem (12:8-10).

Elon

Elon, of Zebulun, was judge for ten years (12:11), but the record tells only that he was "buried in Aijalon in the country of Zebulun."

Abdon

Abdon, of Ephraim, judged Israel for eight years. We only know that he had forty sons and thirty nephews

who rode on ass colts, which was an indication of
his wealth.

Samson

Samson, the thirteenth judge, and last of those listed
in the book of Judges, was by all means the most color-
ful and extraordinary of all. He was the only one born to
be a judge. The Philistines had ruled over Israel forty
years when an angel of the Lord appeared to the wife
of Monoah in Zorah, about fourteen miles west of Jerusalem (13:3). The angel announced that a son would
be born to the woman, and he should be a "Nazarite,"
one dedicated for special service to God. As a Nazarite
the son should abstain from wine or any unclean food
and should allow his hair to grow long.

As Samson matured the Spirit of the Lord moved
upon him and he showed extraordinary strength. Almost immediately, however, he revealed fondness for
Philistines. He married a Philistine woman (14:2), became involved with a Philistine harlot (16:1-3), and
had a fatal affair with a Philistine named Delilah
(16:4-21). Most of his opposition to the Philistines was
prankish or mischievous rather than purposeful assault.
He killed thirty men in Ashkelon (14:19), but this was
the consequence of a riddle told at a party with the
Philistines. As an act of personal spite he tied firebrands
to the tails of foxes and burned the Philistine fields
(15:4, 5). He slew a thousand Philistines with the jaw-
bone of an ass only after his own people arranged his
capture by them (15:11-15). He carried away the gates
of the walls around Gaza, but only after his dalliance
with a woman there (16:1-3).

One writer has observed that "not all of the persons mentioned in the book of Judges were tribal or national leaders. This is especially true of Samson. He led no rising, gathered no army. He did not attack the foe as the champion and deliverer, and even in his prayer for renewal of strength he thinks only of being avenged on the Philistines for his two eyes."

Samson betrayed his Nazarite vows to the scheming Delilah, and was then betrayed by her. Captured by the Philistines, he was blinded and put to work as a beast. Then the Philistines made him into a clown for their entertainment. Samson is included in the register of the faithful (Hebrews 11:32) because in his death he caused the collapse of an idol's temple, which killed "more than they which he slew in his life" (16:30).

Anarchy and Violence

It was a time when "there was no king in Israel, but every man did that which was right in his own eyes" (17:6). This anarchy is summed up in three stories of evil. A young Ephraimite named Micah used money stolen from his mother to make a shrine of household gods (17:5). Micah employed a Levite to be priest of his pagan shrine.

A band of Danites on their way north saw Micah's shrine, stole it and lured the hireling priest away with them (17:16-20). They took the idols and the priest into the country of the Zidonians and set up a shrine there. In the process they attacked the city of Laish and destroyed all the people. The behavior of the Danites violated every higher moral code we recognize today.

The third story tells how a certain Levite's wife was

abused and murdered in the town of Gibeah (19:1-30).
It is an abhorrent account of such perversion, lust and
violence that it created disbelief even in that day. In
grief and anger the husband cut his wife's body into
twelve pieces and sent one part to each of the twelve
tribes to demonstrate what "lewdness and folly" had been
committed in Israel. The result was civil war in which
the innocent suffered more than the guilty, and the
tribe of Benjamin was almost exterminated (20:21). It
was, indeed, a day of anarchy, when "every man did that
which was right in his own eyes."

QUESTIONS FOR REVIEW

1. In the absence of kings, how did God rule His
   people?

2. How many judges were there? Name them.

3. What woman served as a judge? Who assisted her?

4. How did Gideon select his army? How many men
   were finally chosen?

5. What kind of vow did Jephthah make to the Lord?
   What are the two interpretations of his vow?

6. What was a Nazarite?

7. How was Samson chosen to be a judge? What dis-
   tinguished him from the other judges?

8. How did Samson die?

9. Why was the period of the judges a time of anarchy?

"Whither   4
Thou Goest"

Read Ruth 1-4

🎵 The story of Ruth is about what happened to one Hebrew family in the days of the Judges (1:1). It is a simple narrative that tells its own story so clearly that it needs only to be read to be understood and appreciated. The story opens at a time of a great famine in Israel. A man named Elimelech and his family migrated from Bethlehem to Moab, which lay across Jordan to the southeast. The two sons of Elimelech, Mahlon and Chilion, married young women of Moab. For an unexplained reason the father and two sons died, although the fact that the three died so near each other suggests that it may have been an epidemic that killed them.

The widowed Hebrew mother, Naomi, determined to return to Bethlehem. As custom required, her two Moabitess daughters-in-law, Orpah and Ruth, accompanied her to the border of the homeland. Then Naomi told them to turn again into Moab and she would go on alone. Orpah reluctantly turned back but Ruth begged to go on with Naomi. Her words are some of the most beautiful in all literature: "Intreat me not to leave thee, or to return from following after thee: for whither thou goest,

I will go; and where thou lodgest, I will lodge: thy people shall be my people, and thy God my God: Where thou
diest, will I die, and there will I be buried: the Lord
do so to me, and more also, if aught but death part
thee and me" (1:16, 17).

Ruth became spiritually united with the Hebrews and
their God. She would never more serve Chemosh, the
god of Moab, who was worshiped by human sacrifice;
she would hold to Jehovah and His law of love. Because
of her love for Naomi, Ruth would be a part of the noble
succession through whom God's Son would reveal Himself on earth.

Boaz and Ruth

In Bethlehem Ruth helped Naomi glean in the
neighboring wheat fields. As the reapers gathered the
grain some of it always fell to the ground, which poor
people gathered, or gleaned. Ruth worked by chance in
the field that belonged to Boaz, the son of Salmon and
Rahab (Matthew 1:5). This was the Rahab who had
helped the Israelites at Jericho. Boaz loved Ruth immediately, who was evidently already widely known for her
devotion to Naomi, and for her good works (2:11).
When Naomi heard of Ruth's favor with Boaz she
thanked God and revealed to Ruth that Boaz was a near
kinsman to her.

Naomi coached Ruth on how to relate to Boaz. It
was the duty of the next of kin, as Boaz was, to marry
his widowed kinsman and raise offspring in honor of the
deceased. According to custom Ruth needed to make it
known that her days of mourning for her husband were
over and she was ready to marry again. She did this at

the end of the harvest by going to where Boaz slept and lying at his feet. When he became aware of her presence she reminded him of his duty as a kinsman (3:9), and he accepted with pleasure her indication that she would marry him. His desire to marry her was complicated, however, by the fact that there was a nearer kinsman than he (3:12, 13) who might wish to marry her himself.

Boaz negotiated with the near kinsman at the gate of the city. It was customary for the men of the city to do their business transactions at the city gate (Proverbs 31:23), which was usually a large structure with an assembly place nearby. Disputes and grievances were also frequently heard in the gate of the city, for this was an early form of council place, courthouse, or stock exchange.

In the negotiation Boaz made Ruth a part of all Elimelech's property that must be redeemed by the nearest of kin (4:5). The kinsman was unable to redeem the total property, so he forfeited that duty to Boaz, who redeemed it gladly. Now Ruth could be his bride. Boaz took off his shoe, a sign of ownership in those days, to signify that the deal was final. Taking off the shoe was demonstration that the owner could put the soles of his feet on what belonged to him (4:8-10).

By her devotion to Naomi Ruth became an ancestress of Jesus Christ. To her union with Boaz was born Obed, to whom was born Jesse, who was the father of David. Like Rahab, Ruth was a Gentile woman who became part of the royal line of the Hebrews through whom Jesus Christ came to the earth. So, when Jesus was born He was born to all nations of the earth.

QUESTIONS FOR REVIEW

1. Why did Elimelech go into Moab?

2. Who were the women his sons married?

3. In what way did Ruth assist her mother-in-law Naomi?

4. What does the term "gleaning" mean?

5. What kinsman redeemed and married Ruth? Describe how this was done.

6. In what way was Ruth related to King David?

Israel Gets a King

5

Read 1 Samuel 1-31
1 Chronicles 10

The first seven chapters of 1 Samuel are in many way an extension of the book of Judges; they cover a period of transition between the judges of Israel and the establishing of a monarchy. The last two judges, Eli and Samuel who were prominent in this transition, were not like the judges of old, who led Israel in battle. Nor were they like kings, though there were certain regal characteristics in them. They had become permanent civil and social leaders. Judges at this time were something like kings, except that no dynasties were established so that the right of rule belonged to one family, with son succeeding father to the throne.

Samuel was the son of Hannah, a remarkably devout woman, who was barren before his birth. His birth was a miracle for which Hannah prayed (1:10, 11), and because of which she dedicated her child to the Lord (1:28). As soon as Samuel was weaned his mother took him to Shiloh and presented him to Eli, the Judge and High Priest. The devout woman "lent to the Lord" the son for which she had prayed so long. As was sometimes done, the child would grow up in living quarters at the sanctuary and become an attendant to the High Priest. Samuel, like Isaac, Samson and John the Baptist, was born as the result of a miracle, and for a particular purpose.

Eli

The low spiritual and moral state of the times reached even the priest's family. Eli had administered his duties from the sanctuary in Shiloh for forty years. He was what we would call a "good man" but was lazy and weak, indulgent with himself and with his two worthless sons. Despite his piety he was not the moral example he should have been. Eli seemed kind and gentle but he did not set the spiritual pace expected of the high priest. His sons, Hophni and Phinehas, were also priests, yet they were outright wicked, "sons of Belial" who did not know the Lord (2:12). The abuses of the priestly office under these men had brought religion in Israel to a low state of wickedness and contempt. Eli rebuked his sons but it was too late. God sent a man of God to warn the High Priest that judgment was at hand. Hophni and Phinehas would die while they were still young (2:33, 34), and a new and faithful priest would be raised up to take Eli's place.

Samuel

The call of Samuel is one of the most touching spiritual stories in the world. The land of Israel suffered greatly for spiritual guidance: "the word of the Lord was rare in those days; there was no frequent vision" (3:1;

RSV). God called Samuel while he was still a lad to meet that need. Eli, very old and infirm, was asleep when Samuel heard a call which he assumed to be from Eli. Three times Samuel responded obediently to Eli. At last the old priest recognized that it was God speaking to the youth and told him how to respond. God spoke to Samuel and revealed how Eli must be replaced as priest for failing to restrain his vile sons (3:13). Samuel would be the one to replace him. When Eli learned of the prophetic message the following day he humbly accepted the judgment: "It is the Lord: let him do what seemeth him good" (3:18). There was never a trace of resentment or jealousy as the old man watched the youth grow and develop.

Samuel grew physically and in his devotion to God, and became known "from Dan to Beersheba" as a prophet of the Lord (3:20). The term "Dan to Beersheba" is used to express the extremities of Israel: Dan being Israel's most northerly city and Beersheba the farthest south.

"The Glory is Departed"

A new outbreak of war between Israel and the Philistines resulted in Israel's loss of their ark of the covenant. This happened when the Hebrews fared badly in the war and sent to Shiloh for the ark, hoping it would turn the tide of combat in their favor. Instead they lost their most sacred possession to the Philistines. Many Hebrew lives were lost and even Eli's sons were killed in the battle (4:11).

Upon hearing the disastrous news, Eli, ninety-eight years old, blind and very fat, fell in shock and broke his neck (4:15-18). So he and his sons died in one day. The tragedy was still not complete: Eli's daughter-in-law, who was pregnant, went into premature labor and died. The child was named Ichabod, which meant that "the glory is departed from Israel." To this day the word "Ichabod" is used regarding that which has lost its former glory.

Possession of the ark brought the Philistines great harm, as their profanation of the sacred object caused a distressing sequence of misfortunes. The ark was placed in the temple of Dagon, the national god of Philistia, whereupon the idol fell and was shattered (5:1-4). The Philistines were afflicted with tumors (emerods 5:6), very likely caused by an infestation of rats (6:4).

At last the presence of the ark became so unbearable to the Philistines that they arranged for its return to Israel.

Under Samuel's leadership the Hebrews forsook the idolatry they had followed and repented of their sins. This resulted in a stunning military victory over the Philistines (7:10, 11). To commemorate their victory, Samuel set up a memorial stone and called it Ebenezer, saying, "Hitherto hath the Lord helped us."

Israel recovered the cities the Philistines had taken from them and enjoyed a prolonged period of peace. Samuel became the spiritual and civil leader of Israel from his home in Ramah making regular circuit visits to Bethel, Gilgal and Mizpah (7:15-17). He was one of the mountain peaks of Hebrew history, such as Abraham and Moses before him. He wielded an extraordinary influence over the Hebrew nation all his life.

However, when he was old Samuel made the same

error Eli had made, he set his unworthy sons up as judges over Israel. Through the ages many men of vision have been unable to see the sins of their children. Samuel's sons used their office for personal gain; they perverted judgment and abused those who came to them. When offices are inherited rather than earned all manner of evil comes to them. The situation under Samuel's judgeship became almost as undesirable as that of Eli had been. This influenced the children of Israel to demand a king to lead and rule them (8:5). Kings were believed to be persons of glory and power, who would hold the people together and give the nation prominence.

Samuel knew that the demand for a king was a rejection of his rule—and of God's rule. He eloquently warned the people of the tyranny and hardness they would have with a king. Still they persisted; Israel became a monarchy and a new era was born.

Saul

Saul, a tall young man of Benjamin, was chosen to be the first king. When Samuel met Saul (as Saul searched for his father's asses) God revealed to the aged prophet that this was he whom God had chosen to be king (9:17). Samuel anointed Saul privately (10:1), then called all the tribes together at Mizpeh and presented the new king to them (10:20-24). The people accepted Saul gladly, with loud shouts of "God save the king."

Saul was tall and imposing in appearance, every inch a king. He was what the Israelites had dreamed of. Immediately his leadership was tested, for the Ammonites sought to impose a treaty upon the people of Jabesh-

gilead which would require that each Gileadite have one
of his eyes struck out (11:1, 2). The elders of Jabesh
sent word to Saul, who was plowing when he received
the wretched tidings. He thereupon cut up his yoke of
oxen and sent the pieces throughout Israel calling the
people to defend Jabesh-gilead. Any who failed to respond to the call would have his oxen cut up likewise.
An army of 330,000 rallied to Saul and under his leadership defeated the Ammonites. This success led to a
confirmation of his kingship, with a ceremonial en-
thronement in Gilgal (11:14, 15).

Saul's initial success was dimmed when early in his
reign he began to show a spirit of impatience and pride.
He formed a standing army and placed it under the
command of his son, Jonathan. Once when the
Philistines gathered against Israel for battle, Saul became impatient that Samuel was delayed in offering a
sacrifice for victory, so he offered the sacrifice personally
(13:8, 9). This was an intrusion into a function that
only a priest should perform. When Samuel arrived on
the scene in Michmash he rebuked Saul and warned
that this usurpation of divine office would mark the
end of Saul's kingship. His reign would be aborted because of the king's arrogance and self-will.

Jonathan, Saul's son, proved to be an able general, by
defeating the Philistines against great odds. But Jonathan
would never rule over Israel as king, for Saul's continued
independence and disobedience would cost him the
throne. Saul was a man of war, who built a formidable
army of Israelites. He was very successful in battle, and
won victories over many of Israel's foes—Moab, Ammon,
Edom, the kings of Zobah, and the Philistines (14:47,
48, 52).

Saul also went to war against the Amalekites, a people of such evil that God instructed him to put an end to the race (15:3). But Saul again practiced self-will. He exterminated the Amalekite people but spared King Agag (15:8, 9), and, furthermore, he kept some of the spoil he was ordered to destroy. When Samuel confronted Saul about his disobedience the king lied that he had obeyed personally but his troups had disobeyed. He lamely explained that he had spared some of the flocks for the purpose of offering sacrifices.

At this point Samuel said, "Behold, to obey is better than sacrifice," which meant that simply obeying God is better service than all religious ritual (15:22). Saul, by failing to obey God, was rejected as king. Then Samuel executed Agag himself and then departed. The prophet and the king would never again meet officially.

The Rise of David

Samuel's mourning over Saul's failure was both official and personal, for he had held great affection for the young king. His mourning was cut short, however, when God directed him to the household of a Bethlehemite named Jesse, who had eight sons. One of these was to be the next king of Israel (16:1, 2).

God directed Samuel to the youngest and most unlikely son of all, a shepherd named David. The lad was an attractive, ruddy youth, but not of the imposing, regal appearance of Saul. Samuel was reminded that, "Man looketh on the outward appearance, but the Lord looketh on the heart" (16:7). Samuel anointed David in the presence of his family in anticipation of the day he would be king. David was taken to Saul's court where he became an armor-bearer.

From the time of his spiritual failure, Saul gave evidence of a mental disorder, caused by demonic oppression. He was much like what we know today as a manic-depressive, given to frequent deep, dark moods, with other times of excited activity and energy. David was a skilled musician, whose music soothed the rough and dangerous moods of the king (16:23). As David placated the disturbed king with his music he became a favorite of the royal court.

Saul's fondness for David changed to jealousy when he sensed the greatness of David and possibly foresaw his destiny. The first intimation of this was the well-known incident in which David, a lad, killed Goliath, a mighty champion of the Philistines. Israel was at war with Philistia in the valley of Elah, and the giant Goliath repeatedly intimidated the entire Hebrew army with his raging threats. He taunted the Hebrews by challenging them to send one of their warriors to fight him; and that match would determine the outcome of the war. It was a good idea, but who dared to fight the giant? He was over nine feet tall, of such huge size that even his armor weighed 125 pounds (17:4, 5). David went to Elah by chance and while there heard and accepted Goliath's challenge. He used a sling, which he probably used skillfully as a shepherd, and killed the giant before he was in reach of him. In this way the giant's great size and strength were of no use to him.

Thereafter David became a popular hero in Israel, and songs were sung in his praise:

"Saul hath slain his thousands
And David his ten thousands."

Saul was filled with jealousy and rage, even to the point of trying to kill David. The situation was different with other members of the royal family, with whom David had the highest and best of relations. He and Jonathan were stedfast friends, of whom it was said, "He loved him as his own soul" (18:3).

David married Saul's daughter, Michal, who loved David much (18:20, 27). Saul, in his jealousy, hoped the marriage would bring harm to David. As a condition for the marriage he required David to bring him one hundred Philistine foreskins. This was such a dangerous assignment that he thought David would surely fail in it or be killed in the effort. Instead he brought to Saul two hundred foreskins as tokens of his victory over the Philistines. Consequently Saul feared and hated David all the more.

Saul's growing hatred for David erupted into open hostility of such intensity that David, assisted by Jonathan and Michal, had to flee for his life. It is remarkable that Jonathan gave David such love and protection. He was Saul's son and would be king himself one day were it not for David. He would no doubt have made a good king, for he had strong and noble character. David took refuge with Samuel in Ramah until Saul sought him there. Jonathan helped his friend further by revealing to David the determination of his father to kill him, whereupon there remained no course for David but to flee Israel.

David found temporary refuge in Nob with Abimelech, the high priest. No other food was available, so the priest gave David the shewbread to eat (21:6). Because of his assistance to David, Abimelech and eighty-five other priests of Nob were summoned before the mad king and killed.

David, the future king of Israel, then became a wanderer, who took refuge where he could find it. He went even to Philistia and Moab during his period of exile. It is ironic that David was safer among Israel's enemies than he was in his own land. On several occasions he had a chance to kill Saul, but he refused to do so. He said, "God forbid that I should stretch forth mine hand against the Lord's anointed" (24:6, 12; 26:11).

Samuel died during David's exile (25:1), and there was a continued deterioration of Saul's kingship. The end had been seen from the time of his disobedience, and now there was a gradual winding down to the end of Saul's reign. The reign of Saul ended much as it began, in battle against the Philistines. A crucial battle was fought at Mount Gilboa. Saul and his sons, including Jonathan, were among the slain, and their severed heads were displayed as tokens of the Philistine victory. The bodies of Saul and his sons were fastened to a wall in the city of Beth-shan (31:9, 10). The men of Jabesh-gilead, remembering how Saul had defended them at the beginning of his reign, went by night to Beth-shun and retrieved the mutilated bodies. The people of Jabesh fasted seven days in memory of Saul, who could have been a great king.

QUESTIONS FOR REVIEW

1. Who were the final two judges of Israel?

2. What was Eli's failure that led to his rejection?

3. Describe how Samuel was reared as a child.

4. What does the word Ichabod mean? Tell why.

5. What happened to the Philistines when they stole the Ark of the Covenant?

6. Who was Israel's first king? Tell something about his character.

7. Why did God finally reject him from being king?

8. Who was anointed to be the second king of Israel? What was his physical appearance?

9. What did David do in Saul's court?

10. What was the first thing that aroused Saul's jealousy of David?

The United 6

Kingdom

Read 2 Samuel 1-24
1 Kings 1-11
1 Chronicles 11-29
2 Chronicles 1-9

David became king of Israel when Saul died. Under his reign the kingdom was secured and strengthened, and he became the greatest of all Israel's kings. If there was ever a truly ideal period of Hebrew history, it was under the beneficent rule of David. His dynasty was established so strongly that his descendants ruled as long as the kingdom lasted, and it was through his lineage that Jesus Christ was born.

The reign of David, followed by that of Solomon, his son, and the entire Davidic line, is regarded so important to the Hebrew race that it is recorded twice in Scripture (just as the life of Christ is recorded four times). It is recorded first in Samuel and Kings, and then in Chronicles.

David, the King

When Saul and Jonathan were killed in battle an Amalekite rushed to David in Ziklag with the false claim

70

that he had killed them. The messenger believed David would regard this as good news, for it was widely accepted that David would become king when Saul died. Moreover, Jonathan was also dead and any possible hindrance to David's accession to the throne was thereby removed. The Amalekite expected to be rewarded, but he made a fatal misjudgment. David did not regard it as good news, for Saul was his king and Jonathan was his best friend, and he had the Amalekite executed for having killed a king (2 Samuel 1:16).

David went into a period of mourning, which was completely sincere. He had personally spared Saul's life on several occasions, and he never personally harmed a member of Saul's household. David was a profound believer in the divine right of kings, and in the sovereignty of Gods' anointing.

David left his exile in Ziklag and moved to Hebron in the land of Judah, for he himself was of that tribe. In Hebron the people anointed him as their king. One of David's first acts as king of Judah was to reward the men of Jabesh-gilead who had buried the bodies of Saul and his sons. As Saul's first act had been the defense of Jabesh-gilead, so David's first act was to commend them. By his generous attitude toward the household of Saul, David began his reign as king in a positive manner. Such acts of kindness won him the friendship of some who might have been enemies.

At this point one of Saul's captains, named Abner, caused great mischief in Israel. He took Ishbosheth, a surviving son of Saul, and set him up as king of Israel. For two years all of the tribes except Judah were ruled by Ishbosheth, with Abner as his advisor and regent (2 Samuel 2:8-10). With David king in Hebron and

Ishbosheth king in Israel, it was inevitable that there
would be civil war. The war continued with varying in-
tensity for the two years that Ishbosheth ruled over Israel.
Abner, who seems to have been an opportunist, saw that
Ishbosheth would be defeated and defected to David in
Hebron. There he was murdered by David's nephew,
Joab, one of the cruelest men in Hebrew history
(2 Samuel 3:30).

All of this intrigue resulted in the murder of Ishbosheth. When the two men who killed Ishbosheth
brought his head to David in Hebron, David had them
killed, just as he had done to the Amalekite who claimed
to have killed Saul. David's feelings were strong that
none ought to kill or harm the king or the royal family.
This generous treatment of Saul's family strengthened
David in the north and led to his reign over all of
the tribes.

The Tribes Unite

A delegation from the northern tribes came to David
in Hebron and anointed him king over Israel. With this
David became king of all the tribes, and the kingdom
was united in a way it had never been before. He was
thirty years old at the time and reigned over the united
kingdom for thirty-three years. Under the benign rule of
David Israel would become a great nation.

David changed the national capital from Hebron to
Jerusalem. The greater portion of this important city was
still held by the Jebusites, who had founded and occupied it for many years. In fact the name Jerusalem itself
comes from Jebus-Salem, the suffix "salem" meaning
"peace." A section of Jerusalem had been conquered and

occupied by the Hebrews since the days of Joshua (Judges 1:8), but most of the city, especially the area of Mount Zion, proved to be impregnable. David's occupation of the entire city therefore represented a great victory for Israel. It was frequently called the "City of David" (2 Samuel 5:6-9).

The ark of the covenant was brought into Jerusalem so that it became the spiritual center of the nation, as well as its political capital. Almost from the time that David moved to Jerusalem he began dreams and plans to build there a Temple to the Lord. This desire would be denied him, but it would be fulfilled by his son, Solomon. Spiritual man that he was, David was essentially a conqueror and military genius. His skill at war greatly expanded the kingdom of Israel. He won significant victories over neighboring nations and pushed the frontiers outward until Israel became a great and powerful nation.

David performed one further act of kindness to Saul's house. He sought a survivor of the royal household in order that he might do something of honor for Jonathan's sake. It was discovered that Jonathan had a son by the name of Mephibosheth, who lived in the city of Lodebar. Mephibosheth, a cripple who had been injured in his feet when he was five years old (2 Samuel 4:4), was frightened at the first tidings from David, fearing that the new king might want to kill him. David put his mind at ease and then bestowed upon him many honors. Saul's estate was given to him and provision was made for him to be supported from the royal treasury (2 Samuel 9). By such continued acts of kindness, David came to be greatly beloved even by those who had supported Saul.

David and Bathsheba

The account of David's expansion of the kingdom is soiled by a spiritual lapse and sin of the king. The sin was a great stain on the glorious reign of David, and the record of it demonstrates how the sacred Scriptures relate the evil as well as the good of God's people. David's sin occurred when the Hebrew forces were at war with the Ammonites and had the city of Rabbah under seige. David's nephew and military leader, Joab, directed the battle, and David himself stayed behind in Jerusalem. The king had earlier developed an intense physical passion for a woman named Bathsheba, whose husband Uriah was at the siege of Rabbah. David arranged for an illicit liaison with Bathsheba, then endeavored to cover his sin by having Uriah brought home to his wife. When this plan failed, David ordered Uriah to be placed in the battle in such a way that he would surely be killed. The plan was successful and Uriah was killed. David then married the widowed Bathsheba (2 Samuel 11:27).

David committed a sin of massive proportions, especially for one so sensitive and spiritual minded as he. His vile deed would haunt him and bring much grief to his later years.

The Lord revealed David's sin to Nathan, the prophet, who condemned the king with an eloquent parable. He related as fact how a rich man took a poor man's only lamb when he, the rich man, already had many lambs in his fold. David, being the just man that he was, was indignant at the man who would do such a deed and demanded to know who he was. "As the Lord liveth," he said, "the man that has done this thing shall surely die."

"Thou art the man," Nathan said to king David.

David accepted the condemnation and made great repentance; Psalm 51 is the king's poignant prayer for forgiveness. God consoled David that he himself would not die, but the child born to Bathsheba would die. This would be only the beginning of the consequences of his sin. David and Bathsheba had a son named Solomon. This son would succeed his father as king of Judah and Israel. The empire under him would reach its zenith, but the shadow of David's sin would be seen in the tragedy of Solomon's last years.

David's Family

David had numerous wives and those wives bore him many children (2 Samuel 3:2-4; 5:13-16). Amnon, a son of David, became infatuated with his half sister, Tamar, and devised a scheme to make carnal love to her. He pretended to be sick and sent for Tamar to nurse him, and when she came in trust to him he defiled her. After his lustful desires were satisfied Amnon hated Tamar as fiercely as he had once loved her.

When Absalom, Tamar's full brother, heard what Amnon had done to his sister he had Amnon killed (2 Samuel 13:28, 29). Then Absalom fled the country and went into Geshur in the land of Syria. In one convulsion of violence David saw among his children incest, murder and rebellion. It is no wonder that he "wept very sore" (2 Samuel 13:36).

David's greatest sorrow was probably caused by the rebellion of his son, Absalom. This son wished so much to be king that he undermined his father and stole the hearts of the people. He preyed on their emotions by telling them that he would judge in their favor if he were king (2 Samuel 15:2-6). It is easy enough for men who have no authority to tell what they would do if they did have it; they don't have to live with their promises. Those who are willing to resort to Absalom's tactics can become popular very quickly.

Absalom's rebellion against David was culminated when Absalom had himself crowned king in Hebron. Israel was in the sorry position of having son fight against father in open revolt. The tragic and long drawn-out affair was concluded when Absalom was killed. The head of the handsome man was caught in a tree and he was thrust through with swords as he hung there (2 Samuel 18:9-16). When David heard of Absalom's death he wept and said, "O my son Absalom, my son, my son Absalom! would God I had died for thee, O Absalom, my son, my son!" (2 Samuel 18:33).

Seeds of Division

During Absalom's rebellion David had been forced to flee from Jerusalem. Now that the rebellion was ended he was able to return to Jerusalem, where some of his subjects had begun to complain about his absence. With the internal strife at an end, it was hoped that the kingdom might resume its normal course.

Almost by the time David was back in Jerusalem the men of Israel complained that David was giving more attention to Judah than to them. The Israelites accused David of being partial to Judah and there was bitter contention between the two factions (2 Samuel 19:43). As a result of the dispute a Benjamite named Sheba led a revolt of the ten northern tribes against the rule of David.

Joab led the forces of David against Sheba, and be-
sieged him in the city of Abel. There Sheba was killed
and beheaded and his head was carried by Joab to Jerusalem. Even though the revolt of Sheba was shortlived,
it portended the division of the kingdom that was to
come in later years.

Trouble followed trouble as there were other revolts,
after which the land was distressed by famine. The famine came as punishment to Israel because of a massacre
of Gibeonites under King Saul (2 Samuel 21:1). The
Gibeonites got their revenge when seven Israelites were
hanged at Gibeah.

Following the famine there was a new outbreak of war
with the Philistines. The giant Goliath's brother was
killed in this war. This man was also of great stature,
with six fingers on each hand and six toes on each foot.
He defied Israel in the same manner Goliath did
earlier, and it was David's nephew who killed him
(2 Samuel 21:19-21).

David committed a further sin when he took a census
of the Israelites, but his sincerity and devotion to God
moderated his punishment for this. When he was given
the choice of punishment from God or at the hand of
man, he made a statement of devotion that is worth
remembering: "Let us fall now into the hand of the
Lord; for his mercies are great: and let me not fall into the
hand of man" (2 Samuel 24:14). David built an altar
to the Lord and offered sacrifices to Him. It was because of this spirit of worship that David was the greatest of all the kings of Israel.

Accession of Solomon

David's oldest living son, Adonijah, was the logical

choice to succeed his father to the throne. He attempted
to do this, but was unable to establish his claim. The
kingdom went instead to Solomon, David's son by Bathsheba, who was assisted by the prophet Nathan and the
high priest Zadok (1 Kings 1:39). Adonijah recognized
the futility of his efforts to attain the crown and pledged
his loyalty to Solomon. Nevertheless he was ultimately
executed because of royal intrigue.

Under Solomon the united kingdom of Judah and Israel attained its greatest glory and extended its borders
to their farthest limits. The reign of Solomon was com-
paratively peaceful, and he was able to achieve some of
those things his father David had dreamed of doing.

The thing for which Solomon was earliest known was
his wisdom (1 Kings 3:1-28). He began his reign humbly, seeking God for wisdom so that he might rule his
people with divine guidance. God imparted to him a
remarkably diverse gift of wisdom. He exhibited great
insight into human nature when he judged between two
women who claimed the same son (1 Kings 3:16-27).
He was also wise in affairs of state, as he extended his
kingdom through alliances and peaceful negotiation.
This would ultimately lead to his downfall, but it was
basically an effective policy. His wisdom is referred to
in Scripture in the most glowing terms: "And God gave
Solomon wisdom and understanding exceeding much,
and largeness of heart, even as the sand that is on the
sea shore. And Solomon's wisdom excelled the wisdom of
all the children of the east country, and all the wisdom
of Egypt. For he was wiser than all men; than Ethan
the Ezrahite, and Heman, and Chalcol, and Darda, the
sons of Mahol: and his fame was in all nations round
about" (1 Kings 4:29-31).

Solomon was also skilled in literary enterprises. During his lifetime he composed 3,000 proverbs and more than a thousand songs. The Holy Spirit preserved a portion of his proverbs in what we know as the book of Proverbs (Proverbs 1:1). A portion of his songs are preserved in the book we know as the Song of Solomon (Song of Solomon 1:1). The book of Ecclesiastes is also believed to be the product of his understanding (Ecclesiastes 1:1).

The most energetic of Solomon's enterprises was the building of a Temple, and of a royal palace. Solomon was assisted in these efforts by Hiram, King of Tyre, that is Phoenicia, one of the influential kingdoms of that time. The Temple was one of the most splendid structures of all time, with the sanctuary covered with pure gold. Solomon collected taxes and tribute from the nations and peoples subject to Israel in order to finance the magnificent structure.

The splendor of Solomon's kingdom was maintained by a system of heavy taxation exacted during his reign. It is recorded that he had an annual income of 666 gold talents (1 Kings 10:14), which would amount to more than 20 million dollars today. This was an enormous revenue for that time. He created the first navy of the Hebrews (1 Kings 10:22), and a cavalry of 12,000 horsemen and 1,400 chariots. The splendor of Solomon's kingdom was so overwhelming that the Queen of Sheba, a wealthy kingdom of North Africa, was overwhelmed during a state visit to Jerusalem. It was said that, "There was no more spirit in her" (1 Kings 10:5).

Failure of Solomon

With all of the wealth and expansion of Solomon it

seems that his kingdom would have been established for-
ever, but such was not the case. All the time he was
creating material splendor, a spiritual decay was happen-
ing in his own life and in the Hebrew kingdom. The
splendor he created eventually had a greater price tag
on it than the mere gold and silver it had cost. In-
ternational alliances were frequently sealed by royal marriages, so Solomon married many princesses from foreign
countries. During his reign he married 700 women from
various lands, and added to this harem an additional
300 concubines (1 Kings 11:3). It was these wives
who ultimately brought about the downfall of the great
king. They brought their heathen gods into Jerusalem
with them, which right was possibly a condition of the
state marriages. Shrines of worship were built in Jerusalem for many of the gods and the land of Israel became filled with pagan worship.

There was a wide-spread decline in the worship of
Jehovah, and with this decline began a general disinte-
gration of the kingdom itself. Under Solomon the kingdom reached its highest heights, but the seams that held
it together were broken and torn. As the forty-year reign
of Solomon came to a close his kingdom began to fall
apart, with both material and spiritual distress. Heavy
taxation brought the country to a point of revolt and
bankruptcy. Solomon personally engaged in the idolatrous
practices of his wives and led the nation into spiritual
corruption. He who began his reign so wisely ended it
as a fool.

QUESTIONS FOR REVIEW

1. Why did David order the execution of an Amalekite messenger?

2. Who was Ishbosheth?

3. What was the first tribe to make David king? Why do you think they were first?

4. Where was David's first capital? He moved it to what city?

5. Who was Mephibosheth? What did David do for him?

6. What terrible double sin did David commit?

7. What were some of the consequences of David's sin in his own family?

8. Which of David's sons became his enemy? How did he die?

9. Who succeeded David as king? For what things was he famous?

10. What led to the failure of Solomon?

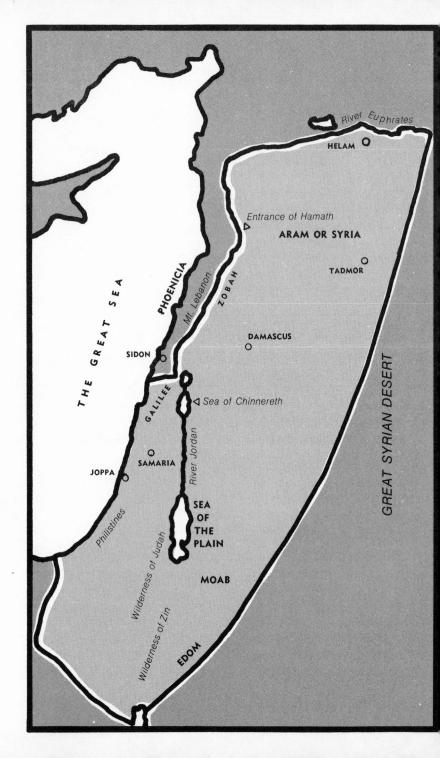

Judah
and Israel

7

Read 1 Kings 12-22
     2 Kings 1-25
     2 Chronicles 10-36

The twelve tribes of Israel were much like the thirteen colonies of America. They began as individual entities, related to one another by heritage, yet each was separate and sovereign within itself. Just as the thirteen colonies were united into one nation, the twelve tribes were welded together as one nation. Saul, David and Solomon painstakingly knitted the separate units into a strong and unified whole.

But there the likeness ends. The American colonies remained unified as a single strong nation, but the Hebrew tribes did not. They were riven, not into a fragmentation of twelve parts, but into two separate nations. The American analogy would have continued if the Confederate State had been successful in the secession so that there were two American nations instead of one. That is exactly what happened in Israel—the united kingdom was divided into two kingdoms of the same Hebrew people.

Even in David's day there were times when the tribe

of Judah stood as one kingdom and the other tribes
constituted a second kingdom. Under Saul and David
the two kingdoms were held together with considerable
success; under Solomon the union was completely successful until dissension arose at the time of his death.

The Nation Is Riven

It is probable that Solomon had many sons, but only
one is mentioned in the Scripture. He was Rehoboam,
the son of an Ammonitess woman, named Naamah (1
Kings 14:31). Rehoboam was therefore half Hebrew
and half Ammonite, and it was for his mother that
Solomon had built a shrine for the god Molech in
Jerusalem (1 King 11:7). Rehoboam had neither the
skills nor the early devotion of his father. He set the
stage for the final rupture between Israel and Judah
when he announced his intention to increase the already heavy taxation begun by his father, Solomon (12:
10-11).

The ten northern tribes chose a man of Ephraim
named Jeroboam, who had been one of Solomon's work
foremen, to be their spokesman in an appeal to
Rehoboam for relief from their heavy burdens. When
negotiations for lighter taxation and other concessions
broke down, Ephraim and nine other northern tribes
withdrew from Rehoboam and the tribe of Judah to form
a separate kingdom. They chose Jeroboam to be their
king (12:16). The tribe of Benjamin remained united
with Judah.

From that time on there were two separate kingdoms

of the Hebrew people: Judah and Benjamin were known as Judah, and the ten northern tribes were known as Israel. Each kingdom had its own king and formed independent alliances with other nations. Frequently the two kingdoms fought together against a common enemy, but they just as frequently went to war against each other. All the kings of Judah were of the line of David, but numerous dynasties reigned over Israel. The ten northern tribes revolted and formed the kingdom of Israel. The ten northern tribes revolted and formed the kingdom of Israel because of their deep jealousy toward the house of David. It was the folly of Rehoboam following the heavy burdens of Solomon that brought the actual rupture, but the seeds of division had existed since earliest times. The tribe of Ephraim was leader in the revolt, for which reason the northern kingdom was sometimes referred to as Ephraim.

Kingdom of Israel

The northern kingdom of Israel got off to a bad start under Jeroboam. He led the nation into apostasy by establishing heathen shrines in Shechem, and there followed him a sorry succession of evil kings. A total of nineteen kings ruled over Israel during about 250 years of its existence. Not one of the nineteen kings was a righteous man; all of them did evil before the Lord. The only change in this depressing monotony was the degree and the extent of their evil.

The following list shows the kings of Israel and the number of years of each reign:

1. Jeroboam	19 years	1 Kings 12:20
2. Nadab	2 years	1 Kings 12:25
3. Baasha	24 years	1 Kings 15:33
4. Elah	2 years	1 Kings 16:8
5. Zimri	7 days	1 Kings 16:10
6. Omri	12 years	1 Kings 16:23
7. Ahab	22 years	1 Kings 16:29
8. Ahaziah	2 years	1 Kings 22:51
9. Jehoram	12 years	2 Kings 3:1
10. Jehu	28 years	2 Kings 9:13
11. Jehoahaz	17 years	2 Kings 13:1
12. Jehoash (Joash)	16 years	2 Kings 13:10
13. Jeroboam	41 years	2 Kings 14:23
14. Zachariah	6 months	2 Kings 15:8
15. Shallum	1 month	2 Kings 15:13
16. Menahem	10 years	2 Kings 15:17
17. Pekahiah	2 years	2 Kings 15:23
18. Pekah	20 years	2 Kings 15:27
19. Hoshea	9 years	2 Kings 17:1

Kingdom of Judah

The kingdom of Judah fared somewhat better than the kingdom of Israel. The kings of Judah were all of the Davidic line, through whom the Lord Jesus Christ would come to the world. Although the kingdom survived 150 years longer than Israel, the same number of kings ruled over each kingdom, which shows that the kings of Judah generally enjoyed longer reigns. Eight of Judah's nineteen kings were righteous men. The list is as follows (with the righteous kings in italics):

1. Rehoboam	17 years	1 Kings 12:17
2. Abijam	3 years	1 Kings 15:1
3. *Asa*	41 years	1 Kings 15:9
4. *Jehoshaphat*	25 years	1 Kings 15:24

5. Jehoram	8 years	2 Kings	8:16
6. Ahaziah	1 year	2 Kings	8:25
7. *Jehoash* .*(Joash)*	40 years	2 Kings	12:1
8. *Amaziah*	29 years	2 Kings	14:1
9. *Azariah (Uzziah)*	52 years	2 Kings	15:1
10. *Jotham*	16 years	2 Kings	15:32
11. Ahaz	16 years	2 Kings	16:1
12. *Hezekiah*	29 years	2 Kings	18:1
13. Manasseh	55 years	2 Kings	21:1
14. Amon	2 years	2 Kings	29:19
15. *Josiah*	31 years	2 Kings	22:1
16. Jehoahaz	3 months	2 Kings	23:31
17. Jehoiakim	11 years	2 Kings	23:36
18. Jehoiachin	3 months	2 Kings	24:8
19. Zedekiah	11 years	2 Kings	24:18

Hebrew Losses

In the south the kingdom of Judah suffered early and lasting defeats. Egypt, under their great general Shishak, overran Judah and its tributary provinces. The Egyptians then proceded northward into Israel and conquered much of the northern kingdom as well. During this same time many of the nations Solomon had won as vassals to Israel were able to pull away and reestablish their independence. The Ammonites, the Philistines and the Edomites were among those lost to the Hebrew empire.

The instability of the period is seen in the constant threat of war that hovered over both kingdoms. In an effort to secure a degree of safety Israel frequently changed its capital, or seat of government. Shechem was first established as capital by Jeroboam. He later changed to the city of Penuel on the eastern side of Jordan (2 Kings 12:25). King Baasha later moved the capital to Tirzah, and then King Omri moved it to Samaria. This remained the permanent capital of Israel. Omri's building of Samaria was as significant for Israel as David's capture and strengthening of Jerusalem had been for Judah. Samaria was built in the hills of central Palestine in a location well-suited for defense.

The capital of Judah never changed from Jerusalem, which remains to this day the heart of the Jewish nation.

Ahab of Israel

The most noted of Israel's nineteen kings was Ahab, the son of Omri. Ahab ruled Israel for twenty-two years and set a new low for wickedness and pettiness. He encouraged Baal-worship in Israel and very nearly brought about a complete departure from the worship of Jehovah. Prodded by his wife, Jezebel, a pagan princess from Phoenicia, he erected a temple to Baal in Samaria. "And he reared up an altar for Baal in the house of Baal, which he had built in Samaria. And Ahab made a grove; and Ahab did more to provoke the Lord God of Israel to anger than all the kings of Israel that were before him" (1 Kings 16:32, 33).

Ahab's pagan queen Jezebel set up a seminary for priests of Baal and supported at least 850 at the expense of the royal treasury (1 Kings 18:19). At the same time the prophets of the Lord were so oppressed that they had to go into hiding. But there was one prophet who did not hide; he was equal to his times.

The Prophet Elijah

A prophet named Elijah challenged Ahab and Jezebel regarding their paganism. He was one of the mountain peaks of Hebrew history, a great man mightily used in

the defense of true worship. The most dramatic en-
counter between the king and the prophet was when
Elijah challenged Ahab to bring the priests of Baal to
Mount Carmel for a confrontation. There at a place of
sacrifice, said Elijah, it would be determined who was
the god of Israel. The priests wearied themselves beseech-
ing Baal to reveal himself and consume the sacrifice.
Elijah prayed to God and immediately the sacrifice was
consumed by a supernatural manifestation of fire (1
Kings 18:38, 39). Then the prophet put the prophets
of Baal to death.

After a long and illustrious ministry, Elijah's life on
earth ended with a spectacular ascent into heaven. A
chariot of fire supported by a whirlwind carried the
prophet away (2 Kings 2:11). He was succeeded by
Elisha, whose ministry in many ways equalled that of
Elijah. These two men demonstrated that God had not
altogether wearied of the sins of Israel.

The Fall of Israel

The kingdom of Israel survived for 238 years. The
kingdom was finally conquered by the Assyrians and
many of the people were carried captive into Assyria
(2 Kings 17:5, 6). With this deportation the people of
the ten tribes virtually disappeared from the history of
Israel, for there is still no record of them as a separate
Hebrew people. The deported Israelites intermarried
with the Assyrians until they lost their identity altogether.

The Israelites who remained in Israel intermarried
with the people around them until they also disappeared
as a separate people. Then the land was populated with
colonists whom the king of Assyria sent from Babylon
and other remote places (2 Kings 17:24-41), and the

Israelites mixed in marriage with these races and mixed their religion with the religions imported from the pagan lands. Gradually the pure-blood Israelites disappeared and in their place there came to be a Mongrel people— half Jew and half Gentile—who were known in the New Testament as Samaritans. These Samaritans would cause Nehemiah trouble in a later time, and by New Testament times they would be utterly despised by the true Jews. A common expression among the Jews of New Testament times was "Thou art a Samaritan, thou hast a devil."

Kings of Judah

The kingdom of Judah existed about 400 years from the time the Jewish nation was divided under Rehoboam. This means that Judah continued alone for 150 years after the fall of Israel.

With varying degrees of faithfulness, eight of the kings of Judah followed the ways of the Lord. The first of these was Asa, who ruled for 41 years. During his latter days, Asa slackened in his early faith, when he is remembered as one who "sought not to the Lord but to the physicians" in his sickness. The physicians were not medical doctors such as we have today, but they treated sickness with a combination of herbal therapy and religious incantation.

Asa's son, Jehoshaphat, also served the Lord. His reign of 25 years coincided with Israel's Ahab, Ahaziah, and Jehoram. Jehoshaphat's godly reign was marred by the marriage of his son, Jehoram, to Ahab's daughter, Athaliah. This daughter of Ahab and Jezebel introduced the Baalism of Israel into Judah. Athaliah herself was a wicked pretender to the throne who actually ruled for one year. During her brief reign she destroyed her own

grandchildren, so that all the royal seed of Judah might
be eliminated and her rule made secure. But one child
was left alive, Joash, who was miraculously spared to
preserve the royal line of David. Joash reigned for forty
years and remained true to God. Other godly kings were
Amaziah, who ruled for 29 years, and Uzziah (also
called Azariah), who ruled more than a half century.

Ahaz

It is possible that the most wicked of Judah's kings
was Ahaz, who ruled for sixteen years. During his reign
he introduced much apostasy to the people, and the
spiritual condition of Judah sank to an all-time low.
Ahaz promoted the worship of Molech, who was worshipped by human sacrifice. An altar to Molech was set
up in the Valley of Hinnom on the southern side of
Jerusalem. This firey altar of death and human sacrifice
ultimately gave the Valley of Hinnom such a bad name
that the Greek word "Gehenna" was derived from it—
and the word "Gehenna" is translated into the English
word "hell."

It was also during Ahaz's reign that the kingdom of
Israel was invaded by the Assyrians who would ultimately destroy them. Ahaz did not lead Judah to war
against Assyria so Judah was spared. The sixteen years
that this evil man sat on the throne were among the
blackest in all the history of the Hebrew people: Israel
in the north was defeated by Assyria and Judah became
almost totally apostate.

Hezekiah

When Ahaz died he was succeeded to the throne by
his son, Hezekiah, who became one of the greatest kings
to sit upon the throne of Judah. For 29 years he ruled

the land in righteousness. He began his reign with a great reformation, in which he cleaned out all the pagan temples and shrines that had been established by his father, Ahaz. Righteousness was reestablished and the worship of God was restored. It was during the good reign of Hezekiah that the prophet Isaiah lived and performed his illustrious ministry. It was also during the reign of Hezekiah that the destruction and deportation of Samaria was completed. As Ahaz had done before him, Hezekiah made peace with Assyria, so that Judah was not destroyed as was the northern kingdom. Judah continued for 150 years after the destruction of Israel.

Probably more than any other king, Hezekiah is spoken of in the Scriptures as a godly king. It is said of him that "Hezekiah had exceeding much riches and honor . . . God had given him substance very much. . . . And Hezekiah prospered in all his works . . . the acts of Hezekiah, and his goodness, behold, they are written in the vision of Isaiah the prophet" (2 Chronicles 32:27, 29, 30, 32).

After Hezekiah, the kingdom of Judah was plunged into evil again. Manasseh had a reign of 55 years, the longest of any king of either Judah or Israel. It is ironic that one of the most godly kings of Judah should be followed by one of the most ungodly. Under Manasseh and his son, Amon, all of the heathen shrines destroyed by Hezekiah were rebuilt. All the great and good works of the godly king were done away.

Josiah

Last of the righteous kings of Judah was Josiah, who ruled for 31 years. During Josiah's reign the Book of the Law was discovered (2 Chronicles 34:14), and the reading of the Law resulted in great reforms in Judah.

Josiah recognized that it was Judah's disobedience to God's Law that had brought great evil upon the kingdom. He therefore called the people together and had the Book of the Law read publicly to them. Then the king instituted with the people a solemn covenant of dedication to God. The Temple was purged and the idolatries of Manasseh and Amon were destroyed. It was a solemn time of great revival, with the reinstitution of the Passover, of which it is said, "There was no passover like to that kept in Israel from the days of Samuel the prophet; neither did all the kings of Israel keep such a passover as Josiah kept" (2 Chronicles 35:18).

The Fall of Judah

When Josiah was killed in battle against the Egyptians, the last godly king died. Those who followed him are only briefly mentioned in the Scriptures; their reigns were very short and their lives were evil.

During the reign of Zedekiah the Babylonians, under the leadership of Nebuchadnezzar, invaded the land of Judah. Judah did not repent or look to God for deliverance—and so the land was destroyed. The Scripture says that "all the chief of the priests, and the people, transgressed very much after all the abominations of the heathen" (2 Chronicles 36:14). God's punishment of Judah was to allow the Babylonians to conquer His people. "They mocked the messengers of God, and despised his words, and misused his prophets, until the wrath of the Lord arose against his people, until there was no remedy. Therefore he brought upon them the king of the Chaldees, who slew their young men with the sword in the house of their sanctuary, and had no compassion upon young man or maiden, old man, or him that stooped for age" (2 Chronicles 36:16, 17).

As Israel had been carried away into Assyria about 150 years earlier, so the finest young men of Judah were now carried away to Babylon. The land itself lay desolate under Babylonian rule, and the enemies of the Hebrews moved in and occupied their land. The best of the people were in exile and those that remained in the homeland deteriorated in both spirit and faith. The Temple was destroyed, as were the walls of the city of Jerusalem. This desolation would continue until God raised up some of those in exile and anointed them to restore the land.

QUESTIONS FOR REVIEW

1. Who was Rehoboam? Who was Jeroboam?
2. Explain how the Jewish kingdom was divided under them. What were the names of the two kingdoms?
3. Who was Jezebel? What evils were the result of her influence?
4. What prophet lived in Israel during the time of Ahab?
5. How many kings ruled over Israel? How many ruled over Judah?
6. How many righteous kings ruled over Judah? How many over Israel?
7. Which of the two kingdoms was the first to be destroyed?
8. Explain how the Samaritan people came into existence.
9. How long did Judah survive after the fall of Israel? What nation defeated Judah?
10. What became of the finest young men of the kingdom?

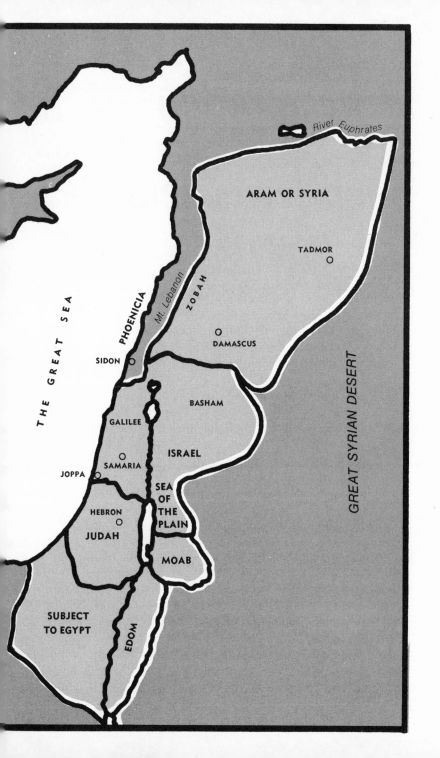

Restoration 8
of Jerusalem

Read Ezra 1-10
Nehemiah 1-13

The books of Ezra and Nehemiah belong to the period of Jewish captivity in the land of Babylon. Along with the book of Esther, these record incidents of Jewish faithfulness in times of national distress. Ezra and Nehemiah are official histories; Esther represents an important sidelight of the mainstream of Hebrew history.

The three books reflect Jewish life in time of extreme difficulty: the Hebrews were either captive in a foreign land or lived in their own land under foreign occupation. These narratives are important because they reveal so much of the Hebrew spirit in the kinds of circumstances the Jewish people have known through the centuries.

The Background

In 587 B.C. Judah was defeated and Jerusalem destroyed by the Babylonians. The finest of the Hebrew people were taken captive into Babylon. After much political and military activity, Babylonia was defeated by

Persia and became a part of the Persian empire. This effected important changes in the lives of the captive Jews. They fared better under Persian rule than they had under Babylonia. The main difference was that under Cyrus of Persia they were permitted to return to their homeland.

To understand the books of Ezra and Nehemiah we need to recall that the ten northern tribes, who were defeated and deported by the Assyrians, intermarried with their conquerors until they became lost to history. All of those who returned in these books were of the tribe of Judah and Benjamin, who comprised the kingdom of Judah before their defeat.

The Jews who remained in Israel at the time of the deportations intermarried with the neighboring races until they became virtually a "mongrel people." These came to be known as Samaritans—half Jewish and half Gentile. There was naturally much conflict between the pure blood Jews that returned from Persia and the half-breed Jews, or Samaritans, who had moved in and occupied the land during the captivity.

Ezra and Nehemiah

Ezra and Nehemiah went from Babylon to Jerusalem at about the same time. The earliest biblical scholars felt that there was evidence that Ezra preceded Nehemiah by about fourteen years, thus the book of Ezra precedes the book of Nehemiah in the biblical canon. Later scholarship, however, is inclined toward the belief that Nehemiah preceded Ezra to Jerusalem. Historical scholars find external evidences that seem to support this view. This is not an important point, only an interesting one.

We know definitely that Ezra and Nehemiah were in Jerusalem at the same time, and their work coincided, for they are mentioned together in the book of Nehemiah.

Ezra's purpose in Jerusalem was religious, and Nehemiah's was civil. Yet both men were of the same mind and had the same zeal for the Lord. Both had been faithful Jews while they were in Babylonia and both were concerned about a restoration of Jewish life in Judea.

The book of Ezra is actually a continuation of Chronicles, as we see in the fact that 2 Chronicles 36:22, 23 and Ezra 1:1, 2 are identical. Approximately fifty years separate the close of Chronicles and the beginning of Ezra. Events recorded in the books of Ezra and Nehemiah cover a period of about one hundred years. The first group of Jews returned to Jerusalem under Zerubbabel in c. 537 B.C., fifty years after the defeat of Judah and the destruction of Jerusalem. A second group returned under Ezra, nearly eighty years later, in c. 458 B.C. Then, another twenty years passed before Nehemiah made the second of his two journeys to Jerusalem, c. 433 B.C.

Return Under Zerubbabel

Cyrus, King of Persia, established a policy permitting the return of captive peoples of his kingdom to their homelands. Under this policy those who had been brought into Babylonia by Nebuchadnezzar were encouraged to return and to carry whatever religious treasures had been brought with them. It is said in Ezra 1:1 that it was the Lord who inspired Cyrus to adopt this policy and proclaim it throughout his kingdom.

Cyrus inquired among the Jews who of them would return to Jerusalem and work toward the building of a Temple to Jehovah. Not all of the captives wanted to return to their homeland, for many had become well established in Babylon and preferred to stay there. The older Jews had been in Babylon for about fifty years and the younger were even born there. These had built up substantial businesses and homes and had no desire to go to Jerusalem. So they gave silver, gold and other properties as a freewill offering for the house of God to those who did wish to return.

Many of the Jews were delighted at the opportunity to return to Jerusalem. King Cyrus restored to them the vessels that had been taken from the Temple by Nebuchadnezzar and the Babylonians. These ancient treasures would be needed for the new Temple.

Zerubbabel and Jeshua were designated to lead the refugees back to Jerusalem. The returning group consisted of 42,360 Jews, with 7,337 servants and 200 singers, for a total of 49,897. They took with them a great number of horses, mules, camels and asses (Ezra 2:64-67). This represented only a remnant of those who had been taken captive to Babylon, but it was a sufficient number to recolonize the homeland.

When the exiles returned home they settled in Jerusalem rather than all of Judah. Conditions in Judah were quite different from the time when they or their parents had left. The people of the surrounding nations had come in and occupied the depopulated territory and the Jews that had remained in the country had intermarried with them. These half-breeds were very friendly with the returning exiles, but the exiles did not return the cordiality. Those who returned had become a different people: they had lived in a strange land and they had learned the lesson of religious isolation. These returning Judeans did not regard the natives of Judah, but those who had been exiles in Babylon as being true Jews.

The returning exiles were afraid of these inhabitants who surrounded them. At this time there was no physical threat or danger, but they were afraid that the inhabitants would corrupt their religion, or that they would attempt to corrupt the race by further intermarriage.

The Restoration Is Begun

Appropriately enough the first thing to be restored was the altar of burnt offerings. This enabled the refugees to resume their daily sacrifices and other religious practices. Next came the task of rebuilding the Temple itself, which since the time of Solomon had been the center of Jewish religious life. If the nation was to be revived then it must begin with the house of God. Materials were secured from Lebanon in the north, whence materials had been secured for the building of the original Temple. When the foundation was completed the event was celebrated with the blowing of trumpets, the singing of psalms of praise, and with the priests in full regalia. For those who could remember the glory of the Temple as it once was, it was a bittersweet experience. The completion of the foundation occasioned in them both rejoicing and weeping, so that it was difficult to distinguish between them (Ezra 3:13).

Samaritan Adversaries

The returning Jews had adversaries with which they

had to contend. These were the Samaritans and other people in the Judean foothills who had profited from the expulsion and deportation of Judah by Nebuchadnezzar. They attempted to hinder the Jews first by subtle methods, and then by overt opposition. (1) First the people went to Zerubbabel and Jeshua and offered to assist them in building the Temple. They claimed to be worshipers of Jehovah and wished merely to be of assistance. Zerubbabel replied that they did not need the help of the Samaritans, but the Jews would build the Temple as had been decreed by King Cyrus.

(2) Frustrated in this attempt, the Samaritans resorted to more overt methods. They drafted a letter to Artaxerxes (or Ahasuerus) who had succeeded Cyrus to the throne of Persia. In their letter the adversaries accused the Jews of promoting rebellion in Jerusalem and Judea. They intimated that if the building should be continued then Persia would lose its hold on Judea (Ezra 4:16). Artaxerxes was sufficiently disturbed by the accusation of sedition and rebellion that he ordered the work stopped. The enemies of Israel gained a temporary victory; for about eighteen years no further building was done.

The Restoration Completed

Haggai and Zechariah were two prophets in Jerusalem at the time. (There is a book of prophecy by each of these men.) They encouraged the work on the Temple to be resumed. Zerubbabel and Jeshua appealed to King Darius, who by that time had succeeded Artaxerxes as king of Persia, for permission to resume the building. They cited the edict of Cyrus, on which authority they had returned to Jerusalem specifically to rebuild the Temple. Darius searched the annals of Persia and found the decree of Cyrus, whereupon he authorized resumption of the building (Ezra 6:1-7).

In about four years the work was completed, the Temple was dedicated, and the Jews celebrated a great Passover feast. Not only did the returning exiles celebrate the Passover, but also the Jews and Israelites who had remained in Judea, upon the condition that they renounce the pagan worship some of them had adopted (Ezra 6:21).

Because the Temple was rebuilt under the leadership of Zerubbabel, it is called in history "Zerubbabel's Temple," which distinguishes it from Solomon's Temple. Zerubbabel was a courageous leader who served as governor of Judea at a most difficult time.

Return Under Ezra

There was a lapse of about fifty years between the completion of the Temple and Ezra's return to Jerusalem. The Bible does not relate what happened during those three generations. Ezra was a devoted student of the Mosaic Law, and seems to have held an important post in the Persian Empire. He is known as a scribe, a name that would later be applied to scholars of the Jewish law. As Ezra became deeply concerned about the spiritual condition of the Jews in Jerusalem he sought the permission of Artaxerxes, or Ahasuerus, to return to Jerusalem. There he hoped to reestablish the Law of Moses as the law of the land. Permission was granted so Ezra led a second contingent of exiles back to Jerusalem (Ezra 7).

A company of 1,500 men with their families accompanied Ezra to Jerusalem. Since his mission was to be essentially a spiritual one, he proclaimed a fast for its success before he left Babylon. The scribe had so assured the king that God would protect them that he was then ashamed to request an armed escort (Ezra 8:22).

When Ezra saw the spiritual laxity of the people in Jerusalem he was grieved at heart. By and large the people had departed from the Law of Moses so much so that it was as if such a Law did not exist. Many of the Jews had married Gentile wives, which had brought a corrupting infusion of pagan cultures and beliefs among the people. Ezra knew that if Israel was to survive as a separate people they must regain their sense of being different from other peoples of the world. His prayer of contrition is most eloquent: "O my God, I am ashamed and blush to lift up my face to thee, my God: for our iniquities are increased over our head, and our trespass is grown up unto the heavens" (Ezra 9:6).

Following Ezra's prayer of contrition many of the Jews were stricken by his sincerity and concern. The widespread response amounted to a spiritual renewal, a renewal of the Jewish covenant with God. The men put away their Gentile wives and renewed themselves as the children of God. Since some of them loved their wives dearly, and had children by them, this reformation came at the cost of extreme personal sacrifice. If this seems rigid or extreme to us today, we must remember that such strict separateness is what has caused the Jews to survive centuries of opposition and oppression.

Nehemiah's Return to Jerusalem

Nehemiah had an influential position in the Persian kingdom, cupbearer to the king. While serving in this position he heard that conditions in Jerusalem were in a sad state. Those who had not been taken captive but had remained in Judea were in great trouble and shame; the walls of Jerusalem were broken down and its gates were destroyed by fire. Nehemiah was so moved by the news that he wept and prayed for the city. His depression lasted for days and he gave himself to constant fasting and prayer before God.

King Artaxerxes observed Nehemiah's sad countenance. In response to his petition the king sent Nehemiah to Jerusalem with letters of recommendation and an escort of horsemen and soldiers. In Jerusalem Nehemiah made a survey of the broken walls. When he told the priests and the rulers of the city that he wished to rebuild the walls they laughed at him and accused him of rebellion against the Persian king. Two influential men from neighboring areas, Sanballet and Tobias, were chief among the scorners and instigated much trouble for Nehemiah.

The Walls Are Rebuilt

Led by the hateful Sanballet and Tobias, the enemies of Israel tried everything possible to prevent the repair of the walls. They tried ridicule (Nehemiah 4:3), armed attack (4:8), physical threats (4:11), and deceptive requests for negotiation (6:2-4). None of their opposition succeeded, for Nehemiah was determined to complete the project. His answer is worth remembering: "I am doing a great work, so that I cannot come down: why should the work cease, whilst I leave it, and come down to you?" (Nehemiah 6:3).

After fifty-two days of work the walls were completed. The inhabitants of the region were disappointed when they saw the completed walls, for they could see that the hand of God was with the returned exiles. The day of their privilege and advantage was over. With the walls completed it was now important to build up the population of pure-blood Jews.

Order Is Restored

Ezra and Nehemiah turned their attention to the spiritual needs of the people. A wooden pulpit was constructed and Ezra the scribe brought forth the scroll of the Law of Moses. The reading of the Law brought about a public confession of sin and iniquity. The general repentance resulted in a spiritual covenant that was written and sealed by the princes, Levites and priests. It is interesting that Nehemiah who was the governor, was the first to affix his seal to the covenant (Nehemiah 10:1).

There was a restoration of order in various aspects of Jewish worship and life. These reforms dealt in particular with the function of the Temple, observation of the Sabbath Day and the sin of intermarriage.

With the city repaired, the Temple restored, and the worship of God renewed, the Hebrew people had hope of rebuilding their nation.

QUESTIONS FOR REVIEW

1. What do the books of Ezra, Nehemiah and Esther have in common?

2. Who was Ezra? Who was Nehemiah?

3. In what way did the Jews fare better under the Persians than they did under the Babylonians?

4. Why was the temple in Jerusalem called "Zerubbabel's Temple"?

5. Who were the Samaritans? Why did they oppose the Jews?

6. Why did Ezra return to Jerusalem? Why did Nehemiah return?

7. What condition of the people in Jerusalem was distressing to Ezra?

8. Who was Sanballet? How did he hinder Nehemiah?

9. What did Ezra read to the people?

10. What effect did it have on the people?

"For Such   9
a Time"

Read Esther 1-10

🕮 Not all of the Jews in Persia returned home under the decree of Cyrus. Many of them stayed in Babylon, where they continued their prosperous businesses, or otherwise continued to lead satisfactory lives in an alien land. This does not mean that they gave up their Jewish way of life, or their devotion to God, which they retained wherever they were.

The story of Esther is about one family that stayed in Persia. The book of Esther does not have anything to do with the mainstream of Hebrew history, it is an interesting account of something that happened in Persia during the time Nehemiah and Ezra were endeavoring to reestablish the homeland in Judea. God is not mentioned anywhere in the book, yet we see everywhere His providential watchcare of His people.

Esther Made Queen

In Ahasuerus' third year as king of Persia, which was about fifty years after the reign of Cyrus, he sponsored a royal festival for the purpose of showing off the greatness of his kingdom. Such pomp and extravagance was common in oriental kingdoms. On the seventh day of the festival, when all the people were reckless through drunkenness, Ahasuerus undertook to display his beautiful queen, Vashti, to the visiting princes. Vashti would not comply with the king's command; she refused to exhibit herself to the stares of the drunken men. Noble and admirable as her standards might have been, her denial of the king's request led to her dethronement. No doubt she was aware of the consequences of her refusal, but she would rather be dethroned than expose herself before the lustful gazes of the men.

God used the dethronement of Vashti for His own purposes, for her successor as queen was a young Hebrew girl named Hadassah, more commonly known as Esther. Esther was selected from among all the maidens of the kingdom to be the new queen. She was the foster daughter of Mordecai, a Benjamite. The two were actual cousins, but Mordecai, an older man, was Esther's guardian. He was an official in the king's court, probably a warden of the eunuch's quarters, in which position he gained information about a plot to kill the king. He revealed the plot to Ahasuerus, and thereby gained the king's appreciation.

Another man of considerable influence with the king was Haman, an Agagite, who fiercely hated the Jews. This hatred came to a murderous boil when Mordecai refused to bow to Haman. Haman therefore engineered a plot to have the Jews put to death. On a certain day selected by lot, all the Jews of the kingdom would be killed. Haman was one of a long line of evil men through human history who have endeavored to exterminate God's people.

Esther's Intervention

Upon hearing of Haman's plan Mordecai appealed to Esther for help. He perceived that God had ordained Esther's position as queen for the very purpose of "preserving her people." He said, "Who knoweth whether thou art come to the kingdom for such a time as this" (Esther 4:14).

Esther was afraid to go to the king without his invitation. To approach the king without being invited was a crime worthy of death. Ahasuerus received Esther, however, whereupon she invited him and Haman to a banquet in her quarters. At Esther's banquet the queen revealed Haman's plot to kill the Jews. Ahasuerus was filled with wrath and ordered the execution of the man who had devised such evil against the Jews. Ironically Hamon was hanged on the very gallows he had prepared for the execution of Mordecai (Esther 7:10).

Persian law was such that Ahasuerus could not annul what he had earlier decreed. So he made a second decree that counteracted the first: he sent documents throughout the kingdom authorizing the Jews to arm themselves and to resist those who might endeavor to kill them. Because of the marvelous way God intervened for the Jews, many of the people of the land accepted the Jewish faith (Esther 8:17). The Jews celebrated their deliverance with a great spiritual feast.

The Feast of Purim

Haman had cast lots, called Pur, to decide the day the Jews were to be killed. Using a play on the word, Pur, Mordecai named the feast the Jews celebrated,

Purim. This became an annual feast, at which in later years the Jews always read the book of Esther.

The book of Esther is filled with ironies: Haman was hanged on the gallows he devised for Mordecai; the officials who were originally authorized to execute the Jews ended up helping them; instead of the Jews being wiped out they were increased, for many of the Persians were won to their religion. It is interesting to go through the book of Esther and pick out all of the ironies in which God turned the evil designs of man into the benefit of His people.

The story of Esther is a beautiful account of God's watchcare over Israel. It tells men of all generations and races that God moves on behalf of His people in ways that they do not always understand. He brings to defeat the evil that is devised against His children, and then lifts them to a safe and honored place.

QUESTIONS FOR REVIEW

1. Who was Vashti? Do you regard her response to the king as good or bad?

2. Who was Hadassah? By what other name was she known?

3. Why did Mordecai think Esther was chosen queen?

4. For what great evil is Haman known?

5. In what way were the Jews given protection from their enemies?

6. What does the Feast of Purim celebrate?

INSTRUCTIONS FOR PREPARING
A WRITTEN REVIEW

1. A Certificate of Credit will be awarded when the student satisfies the requirements listed on page 7.

2. The student, at a time designated by the instructor, should prepare the written review following the guidelines listed below. The student should use blank sheets of paper and make his own outline for the review. The completed written review should be presented to the instructor for processing.

3. In the case of home study, the student should present his answers to the pastor or to someone whom the pastor may designate.

HIGHLIGHTS OF HEBREW HISTORY

By Charles W. Conn

CTC 203—Written Review

1. Name the twelve historical books.
2. Write a short paragraph on why the historical books are important to us.
3. Do you think Joshua was a good successor to Moses? Write two reasons for your answer.
4. What similar miracles marked the beginning of the Hebrews' journey and its end? How were they different?
5. Prepare a list of the fifteen judges.
6. Write a brief paragraph on your favorite judge.
7. Do you think Samson did all that was possible to help the Hebrew people? Give the reason for your answer.

8. Who was Ruth? What do you think was her most commendable characteristic?

9. What was the young David's attitude toward King Saul?

10. Why do you think Saul was jealous of David?

11. What city did David make his capital? What was the meaning of the city's name?

12. What did the prophet Nathan mean when he told David the parable of the king who stole the poor man's lamb?

13. Name some of the ways that David suffered for his sin.

14. Explain how the United Kingdom was divided into two separate kingdoms.

15. Name at least three of the righteous kings of Judah.

16. Discuss some of the incidents in the life of the prophet Elijah.

17. Write a short paragraph on how the Samaritan people came into existence.

18. What became of the ten Jewish tribes that were carried away into Assyria?

19. From what Hebrew tribes do the people come whom we now know as Jews?

20. What was "Zerubbabel's Temple"?

21. In what way did Ezra and Nehemiah do a similar work? In what way was their work different?

22. From the book of Nehemiah, list some of the ways enemies try to hinder the work of the Lord.

23. What particular sin of the Jews did Ezra condemn? Why is that important to the Jews of today?

24. Explain how God worked for His people in the episode of Vashti and Esther.

25. What lessons are we able to get from the story of Esther?